POLYNESIAN PANTHERS

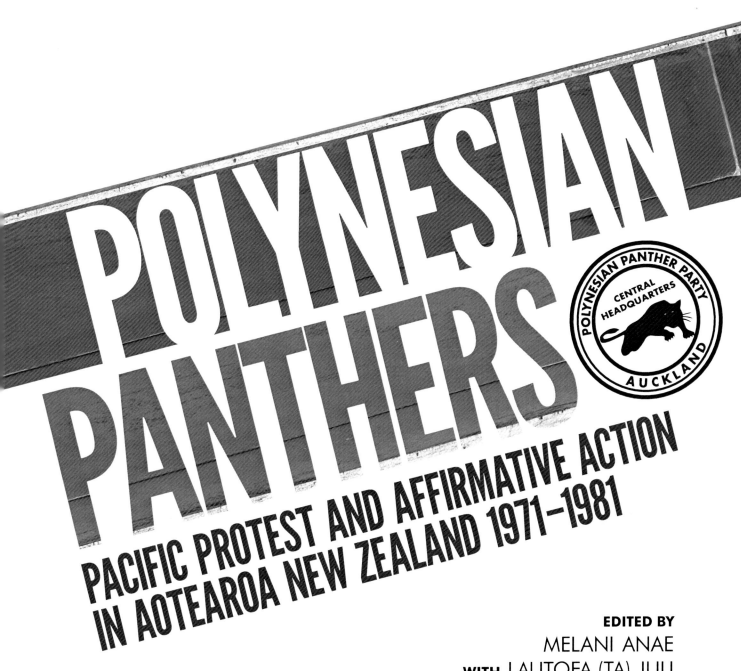

POLYNESIAN PANTHERS

POLYNESIAN PANTHER PARTY
CENTRAL HEADQUARTERS
AUCKLAND

PACIFIC PROTEST AND AFFIRMATIVE ACTION IN AOTEAROA NEW ZEALAND 1971–1981

EDITED BY
MELANI ANAE
WITH LAUTOFA (TA) IULI
AND LEILANI TAMU

HUIA

First published in 2006 by Reed Publishing (NZ) Ltd

This edition published in 2019 by Huia Publishers

with the support of Whitireia Publishing.

Huia Publishers

39 Pipitea Street, PO Box 12280

Wellington, Aotearoa New Zealand

www.huia.co.nz

ISBN 978-1-77550-205-0

Cover and internal design: Leon Mackie

Cover photo: © John Miller 1971

Back cover quote: Newton, H. P. (1974) *Revolutionary Suicide*. London: Consolidated Productions and Wildwood House, p.14.

Published with the assistance of Te Whare Kura Thematic Research Initiative, University of Auckland.

CONTENTS

VI   **KEY EVENTS 1971–1981**

XIII   **FOREWORD**

XVI   **ACKNOWLEDGMENTS/FA'AFETAI**

XVIII   **INTRODUCTION**

1   **PART ONE:** FROM FALEALILI TO PONSONBY

13   **PART TWO:** THE 'NEW ZEALAND-BORN' EXPERIENCE

27   **PART THREE:** PONSONBY – THE 'LITTLE POLYNESIA IN NEW ZEALAND' – AND THE GANG EXPERIENCE

47   **PART FOUR:** FROM GANG TO POLYNESIAN PANTHER MOVEMENT

87   **PART FIVE:** FROM POLYNESIAN PANTHER MOVEMENT TO POLYNESIAN PANTHER PARTY

99   **PART SIX:** 'ONCE A PANTHER, ALWAYS A PANTHER'

119   **PART SEVEN:** THE LEGACY OF THE POLYNESIAN PANTHERS

124   **APPENDICES**

145   **GLOSSARY**

149   **ABOUT THE EDITORS**

150   **INDEX**

KEY EVENTS 1971–1981

1971

JUNE–AUGUST

The Polynesian Panther Movement (PPM) organises and runs events such as Earth Day and bottle drives.

5 JUNE

A gang riot takes place in Symonds Street, Auckland.

16 JUNE

The PPM is officially set up.

3–4 JULY

PPM carries out its first act as a group: helping out with cooking and ticket collecting at the New Zealand University Students' Association Arts Council Rock Festival.

EARLY AUGUST

Four PPM members walk into mayor Sir Dove-Myer Robinson's office seeking help to set up club headquarters in Ponsonby. They receive a warm reception from the mayor and his committee.

SEPTEMBER

PPM publishes its initial 'Platform on Movement Positions and Structure of the Organisation'.

22 SEPTEMBER

PPM helps to set up a Youth KLUB in Ponsonby, which was made up of former APACHE gang members.

26 SEPTEMBER

PPM plans and organises the first of several outings for senior citizens.

7 OCTOBER

PPM meets with Auckland city councillor Tom Tahu to discuss plans to establish a community hall for local youth.

9 OCTOBER

PPM hosts and organises a social held at the Ponsonby Community Centre.

20 OCTOBER

PPM receives several positive responses from the community, as published in the *West End News*.

LATE 1971

PPM protests against the New Zealand men's softball team's upcoming (February 1972) tour of South Africa.

PPM sets up its headquarters at 315 Ponsonby Road.

1972

26 JANUARY

PPM organises local support for a worldwide petition calling for the United Nations (UN) to investigate the death of George Jackson, a black prisoner who was shot dead by prison guards in the United States.

3 MARCH

An interview with PPM members Will 'Ilolahia, Henry Neenee and Nooroa Teavae is published in *Socialist Action*. PPM is described as 'a revolutionary organisation for the Polynesian community' with five chapters in the Auckland area.

15 MARCH

Community meeting organised by the Polynesian Education Foundation Fund-Raising Committee.

A PPM member is elected to sit on the executive of Pacific Islanders (New Zealand) Association.

22 MARCH

A sit-in demonstration is held at New Lynn Shopping Centre in protest at the closing of Avondale's only Saturday night dance. The sit-in has been organised jointly by Ngā Tamatoa Council, PPM and the Stormtroopers.

25 MARCH

PPM and the People's Union organise the first weekly bus service for visitors to Paremoremo, Auckland Maximum Security Prison.

29 MARCH

PPM, Ngā Tamatoa, the Stormtroopers, Head Hunters and Tihei Mauriora come together to form 'a loose Polynesian Front'.

12 APRIL

Will 'Ilolahia speaks to students and staff at North Shore Teachers College about the realities faced by Polynesian students in the New Zealand educational system.

21 APRIL

PPM organises and supervises the Ponsonby Street Dance, which is attended by 3000 people.

3 MAY

Ama Rauhihi is appointed PPM minister of culture and attends an 'Inward Bound' scheme organised by Ngā Tamatoa and held at Tokomaru Bay.

22 MAY

PPM and the People's Union organise a community food programme to help those who are suffering as a result of rising food prices.

14 JUNE

PPM minister of information Wayne Toleafoa publishes an article in the *West End News* to 'clear up some of the misconceptions some of the community hold concerning PPM'.

Will 'Ilolahia is elected as one of the three vice-presidents of the Pacific Islander (New Zealand) Association.

21 JUNE

PPM organises a weekly education centre at 24 Williamson Avenue, Grey Lynn.

23 JUNE

PPM participates in a South African Freedom Day demonstration.

KEY EVENTS 1971–1981

30 JUNE–7 MARCH 1973

PPP sell more than 600 copies of a booklet on citizens' legal rights.

3 JULY

Will 'Ilolahia speaks at the University of Sydney.

5 JULY

Will 'Ilolahia is invited by Bobby Sykes, Australian black civil rights leader, to attend a Black moratorium in Sydney on 14 July 1972.

13 JULY

PPM plans and organises a solidarity demonstration in Auckland.

14 JULY

PPM takes part in and is one of the many supporters of the protest march against the Vietnam War.

Will 'Ilolahia is arrested in Sydney during an Aboriginal rights march.

30 JULY

Will 'Ilolahia announces that plans are underway for 'solidarity and cooperation' between PPM, Aborigine Black Power groups and Black Power supporters in Papua New Guinea.

2 AUGUST

Will 'Ilolahia returns from a three-week speaking tour during the Australian Black moratorium. He has spoken in Sydney, Melbourne, Canberra and Brisbane.

1 SEPTEMBER

Minister of Māori Affairs, Mr MacIntyre, states that he would like to 'nail' rack-renters exploiting Māori and Polynesian peoples in Auckland.

9 SEPTEMBER

PPM receives positive publicity in an article published in the *New Zealand Herald* detailing its emergence and ideologies.

19 SEPTEMBER

Mayor Sir Dove–Myer Robinson presents PPM with the governor general's youth award, $250 (granted jointly with Ngā Tamatoa) and a special commendation for the Hillary College Polynesian Club.

13 OCTOBER

A PPM member is wrongfully arrested by two police constables outside a school dance held at Seddon High School.

NOVEMBER

PPM changes its name to Polynesian Panther Party (PPP) 'with a new structure, tactics and whole new attitude' in relation to its work.

1 NOVEMBER

PPP selects their minister of culture Ama Rauhihi to become their full-time community worker from 1973.

6 DECEMBER

Three American black clergymen visit Ponsonby to meet with Polynesian peoples and give them 'valuable advice on fund-raising, organising, community programmes, welfare and political work'.

13 DECEMBER

PPP appeals for donations from the local community to help employ Ama Rauhihi as its full-time community worker.

20 DECEMBER

PPP member Mary Meanata returns from Tonga after teaching there for 11 months under the Volunteer Service Abroad scheme.

DURING 1972

PPP lobbies Auckland City Council to put in traffic lights at an accident-prone pedestrian crossing on Franklin Road.

1973

9–11 FEBRUARY

Ama Rauhihi speaks at the AGM of the New Zealand Race Relations Council.

EARLY APRIL

PPP receives a $1,000 grant for social services to Polynesians in Auckland from the National Council of Churches.

6 APRIL

The *City* and *West End News* offer to donate $5 per week towards financing a full-time PPP social worker.

7 APRIL

Members of PPP attend a Citizens Association for Racial Equality (CARE) seminar on 'Justice and Race' held at the Unitarian Church, Ponsonby.

11 APRIL

PPP and Ngā Tamatoa put forward candidates to stand for the Seddon High School board.

18 APRIL

PPP writes to the editor of the *Sunday Herald* to complain about its recent description of a fight between Tongan and Māori youths in Onehunga as 'racial warfare'.

5 MAY

PPP organises and runs another Ponsonby Street Dance.

23 MAY

PPP sends clothes and donations to help Mr Sefo Hola (a Tongan citizen) who deliberately delayed a French aircraft for one and a half hours during French nuclear bomb tests in 1972.

6 JUNE

PPP begins a rent strike against its landlord on the grounds that he had not lived up to his responsibilities to maintain the building.

17–19 JUNE

Will 'Ilolahia and Bill Bates travel to Christchurch to set up a PPP solidarity committee, make people more aware of race problems and to raise funds for their various social aid programmes.

KEY EVENTS 1971–1981

JULY

Ama Rauhihi attends a resourcement conference in Kuala Lumpur and the People's Forum in Singapore. She is also selected as one of four members of a Māori delegation to study Chinese minority groups in China.

11 JULY

PPP and CARE run an informal homework centre in the Ponsonby parish of Father Birch.

12 JULY

In an article in the *New Zealand Herald*, University of Auckland sociology lecturer A J C Macpherson supports the PPP and urges the public to listen to its message.

JULY–AUGUST

PPP member Norman Tuiasau attends the tenth International Youth Festival in Berlin, Germany.

17 AUGUST

PPP plans for a homework centre for Polynesian and Māori children living in Dunedin.

11 SEPTEMBER

PPP and Ngā Tamatoa organise and support National Māori Language Day.

20 SEPTEMBER

A PPP member is accused of robbing a Japanese captain at a party in Ponsonby, but he denies he was involved.

10 NOVEMBER

PPP sets up a Tenants' Aid Brigade as a part of its community programme to help tenants faced with illegal eviction from their homes.

Will 'Ilolahia is arrested and charged with assault after a fight at a party.

20 NOVEMBER

PPP is reported to have plans to open new branches in South Auckland and have two full-time community workers before the end of the year.

24 NOVEMBER

PPP and the People's Union organise a demonstration outside Paremoremo Prison to support the life-prisoners in D-block who are striking over the inhumane conditions there.

6 DECEMBER

A meeting is held at the Young Women Christian Association (YWCA) in support of the three prisoners at Paremoremo Prison who have ceased their 14-day hunger strike.

22 DECEMBER

PPP organises and hosts a Christmas party at the Māori Community Centre.

1974

JANUARY

PPP puts out its PANTHER platform and programme.

25–27 JANUARY

A meeting is held 'amongst all Māori and other Polynesian progressive organisations to form a United Front for 1974'.

JANUARY–FEBRUARY

Will 'Ilolahia is charged with assault and PPP begins a defence campaign to raise funds for his legal costs.

20 FEBRUARY

PPP receives a letter of support from the New Zealand Student Christian Movement and New Zealand Race Relations Council, support and solidarity for PPP's struggle for justice.

27 FEBRUARY

Members of PPP travel to Wellington to present a submission from the Auckland Committee on Racism and Discrimination to a Parliamentary Social Services Committee examining the Children's and Young Persons' Bill.

4 MARCH

PPP members and Auckland Committee on Racial Discrimination appear before the Parliamentary Social Services Committee for a second time.

24 AUGUST

PPP and the People's Union protest outside a landlords' meeting (attended by Robert Muldoon) against evictions, high rents and poor conditions.

31 AUGUST

PPP is reported to have been involved in demonstrations outside parliament.

SEPTEMBER–OCTOBER

PPP organises a Prisoners' Aid Programme, which includes writing letters to prisoners. An interview with PPP members Will 'Ilolahia and Billy Bates is published in the *Black Panther* (United States).

13 SEPTEMBER

PPP, the Ponsonby People's Union, ACORD, CARE, and Ngā Tamatoa set up Police Investigation Group (PIG) patrols to monitor the oppressive tactics of the Police Task Force.

1975

JANUARY–FEBRUARY

PPP prints the first edition of its newspaper, the *Panther's Rapp*, 'to give a true picture that will represent the Polynesians' interests and their true identity'.

13 JUNE

PPP organises a fund-raising social at the University of Auckland.

KEY EVENTS 1971–1981

14 SEPTEMBER
PPP participates in and organises solidarity activities to support the land march organised by Te Roopu o te Matakite.

29 SEPTEMBER
PPP plans on sending a letter of complaint to the minister of police about a 'concerted police effort to harass PPP members and supporters'.

1976

EARLY JANUARY
The police raid PPP headquarters.

16 JUNE
PPP organises a weekend conference to discuss and confront the social problems suffered by Polynesians in Auckland.

21 NOVEMBER
Auckland City Council notifies PPP that its new office will be demolished to make way for a car park.

1977

17 FEBRUARY
In light of the planned demolition of PPP's headquarters, Tigi Ness states that 'members will refuse to leave the house until the council found them alternative accommodation'.

26 FEBRUARY
Panthers stage around-the-clock sit-in at their Ponsonby headquarters in protest at the demolition plans.

19 MARCH
Auckland City Council is reported to be considering the option of subsidising PPP's rent at its new Ponsonby headquarters.

1978

20 APRIL
Will 'Ilolahia is nominated by the National Youth Council for the New Zealand Social Services Council, but the government rejects the nomination because of his political and criminal background.

1981

12 SEPTEMBER
PPP participates in a Patu Squad protest against the 1981 Springbok Tour at Fowlds Park in Auckland. This was their last 'official' act as a group, although the Panthers never disbanded and continue today.

FOREWORD

FROM DAVID HILLIARD
FOUNDING MEMBER AND
CHIEF OF STAFF OF THE
BLACK PANTHER PARTY, USA

The vision of the Black Panther Party is expressed by its founder and leader Huey P Newton through its philosophy, Revolutionary Intercommunalism. Revolutionary Intercommunalism is an idea which emerges out of a fundamental contradiction: that America is not a nation but an empire which directly or indirectly spans the globe, that its real units are communities which are ever more visible as one goes down into the Third World strata of America, and that empire and community empire than that man should live in a community which escapes the manipulation of the rulers. The villages of the world have much to teach its cities. 'We cannot make our stand as nationalist, for the closer one is to the center of the empire, the more illusory the idea of nationhood is for any people. 'We cannot even make our stand as internationalist' for an aggregate of citizens of the world is little more than an aggregate of bourgeois individualists. We must place our hope on the philosophy of

"... the program of the Polynesian Panther Party (PPP), based in Auckland, New Zealand, is strikingly similar to that of the Black Panther Party. Last week, THE BLACK PANTHER presented Part I of [an] interview, which describes the PPP's philosophy, program and continuing struggle to organize oppressed Polynesians to transform their society." [1]

stand in dialectical contradiction and confrontation with each other ... The Third World in America can never become a part of the American nation because there is no nation. To become a part means joining the empire which for most Third World people means to do so in a menial capacity. Third World people live in communities not by choice but because they are forced to remain in demarcated ghettos. Millions of white Americans live not in communities but as atomized individuals and in households. Nothing is more natural to man than to live in a community, but nothing is so abhorrent to the doctrines of 'freedom' of the intercommunalism – only those who are by, through and from the community can serve the great family of humankind. To go out one must go deep, but to go deep, one must go out.' [2]

By the mid-1970s, the party had reached its pinnacle of influence. Huey was the pre-eminent African-American leader for social justice in the world, with the Panthers counting over forty chapters domestically, as well as chapters in England, Israel, Australia, India and Auckland (New Zealand's Polynesian Panther Party). In addition to political coalitions with liberation movements overseas, unions were established among Asian American,

FOREWORD

Latinos, white peace activists, feminists, lesbians and gay men in the United States.

Fundamental to our work of this period was Huey's renewed call for institution building. Although this feature had been central to the ideological platform laid in the Ten Point Program in 1966, we had strayed from our original purpose. Eldridge Cleaver, for example, had alienated the Black Panthers from many in the community programs. Through this influence we helped to elect progressive political candidates, including Party members, who now sat on public school-boards and other positions of regional and national authority. As a result, critics soon charged Huey with 'selling out' the movement to the very system from which the panthers had previously demanded independence. In reply Huey invoked intercommunalism by way of explanation. 'I contend

"Last week, the Black Panther Party received a very warm and sincere message of solidarity from the Polynesian Panther Party based in Auckland, New Zealand. Accompanying that letter were informational materials, including ... the ongoing organisational efforts on the part of the Panther Party to transform their society into one which meets the needs and desires of the Polynesian community." [3]

who did not relate to his either/or 'philosophy of revolution now'. Moreover, Eldridge had abandoned the Survival Programs during Huey's absence while he was incarcerated, leading to further breaches in support where those ties were most essential: namely, between the party and people living in local communities where we were active. Reclaiming the politics of empowerment as our keystone, the Black Panthers now exercised considerable strategies to transform the American establishment: lobbying on behalf of the poor to secure thousands of jobs, low-cost housing and public funding to operate the free community that no one is outside the system. The world is so close now, because of technology, that we are like a series of dispersed communities, but we are all under siege by the one empire-state authority, the reactionary inner circle of the United States'. [4]

**All Power To The People,
David**

ENDNOTES

[1] Excerpt from *The Black Panther*. USA, 5 October, 1974.

[2] Excerpt from Newton, H. P. (1972) *To Die for the People*. New York: Random House.

[3] Excerpt from *The Black Panther*. USA, 28 September, 1974.

[4] Excerpt from Hillard, D. (2006) *Huey: Spirit of the Panther*. New York: Basic Books.

ACKNOWLEDGMENTS/FA'AFETAI

Firstly we acknowledge Huey P. Newton for his inspiration and the Black Panther Party for their ceaseless efforts to alleviate the oppressed. The idea for this book was born on June 2001, at the 30th anniversary of the Polynesian Panther Party. This is not the definitive book on the Polynesian Panthers, for there are many stories that cannot be printed, but it will lead the way for the other stories to be told, in other ways. On behalf of the editorial team, myself Ta Iuli and Leilani Tamu, I would like to thank the following whose contributions form the heart of the book – Panther members: Will 'Ilolahia, Panther Twenty-nine, Wayne Toleafoa, Alec Toleafoa, Tigilau Ness, Nigel Bhana, Etta Gillon (née) Schmidt, Fuimaono Norman Tuiasau, Victor Tamati, Billy Bates, Ta Iuli, Vaughan Sanft, Aloma Wehi, Elizabeth Meanata, Mapu Iuli, Mere Meanata-Montgomery, Sally Atiga, Lenora Noble, Fa'amoana 'Foof' John Luafutu, Misatauveve Melani Anae and Vincent Tuisamoa; investigators: The Shillouette Sam Sefuiva; and supporters: Ness Sesega, Ngā Tamatoa, Hone Harawira, the late Hon. David Lange, John Harris and Michael Hart (City & West End News), Robert Ludbrooke (NLO), Roger and Lyn Fowler (People's Union), Tom Newnham (CARE) and Joris de Bres (CARE). Fa'afetai, fa'afetai, fa'afetai lava.

For the technical aspects of the book, in particular the researching and digging out of the archival material and images, and boundless enthusiasm and energy during the last stages, a special thanks goes to Leilani Tamu. Fa'afetai lava to Will, Etta, Nigel and Roger, for their photo and archival material, and to Ta for his assistance in gathering some of the interviews and stories. We are extremely grateful to Front of the Box Productions, Waiata Artist Trust, Māori Television, and Rachel Jean and Damon Fepulea'i of Isola Productions for making documentary footage available to us. Fa'afetai also to the Macmillan Brown Centre, University of Canterbury for giving us permission to reprint excerpts from *A Boy Called Broke*. We also acknowledge Michael Fonoti Satele who wrote an MA thesis on the Polynesian Panthers in 1998.

Finally, we thank those to whom we owe the most. We acknowledge our Pacific ancestors who initiated our voyages across the Pacific over space and time. Then there are also our grandparents and parents who were brave enough to forge pathways to New Zealand in order that their children, grandchildren and New Zealand-born generations to come would have a better life, in the hope that in doing so, they would still maintain links to their Pacific cultures, their homelands and their transnational corporations of kin.

Our final thanks go to the children and families of the Panthers who have patiently put up with so much of our radical behaviour in the past (and now?), and who finally, we hope can reap the benefits of what we fought for and tried to achieve. It is up to you, our children and other Pacific youth, to continue the legacy of our ancestors. Power to the People!

The book is dedicated to those Panthers who have passed on – Captain Fred Schmidt, Jimmy Marsh, Betty Neenee, Tom Hodges, Bill Hodges, Nooroa Teavae, Big Ed – Eddie Williams, Sam Iavakeiaho Vete, Paul Dapp and Gordon Stanley. Others remembered are Agnes Tuisamoa, Rev. Leuatea Sio, Sandy Edwards, Tom Newnham and Cecil Fowler. You will always be remembered. We will also remember those other Panthers, investigators and supporters whose names are mentioned in this book, but whose stories still remain silent. Seize the Time!

Yours in solidarity,
Misatauveve Dr Melani Anae

INTRODUCTION

A brief summary of the contents of the book

Polynesian Panthers covers an era from the founding of the Polynesian Panther Party (PPP) in 1971 – inspired by the American social consciousness and advocacy group, the Black Panthers – to their last public act, a Springbok tour protest in 1981.

In the 1970s, the Polynesian Panthers had to engage simultaneously with two dominant groups – Māori, the indigenous people of Aotearoa who were embroiled in a sovereignty movement against white supremacism and the colonial dispossession of Māori taonga, and Palagi racial discrimination and exploitation that met Pacific peoples upon their migration to New Zealand.

The Panthers undertook a variety of grassroots activities – some in partnership with their Palagi equivalent in Ponsonby, the People's Union – including: organising prison-visit programmes and sporting and debating teams for inmates; providing a halfway house service for young men released from prison; running homework centres; and offering interest-free 'people's loans', legal aid, and food banks that catered for 600 families at its height.

The PPP developed and pursued survival strategies for Pacific peoples against racism and colonialism and thus provided the most explicit and intentional articulation in Aotearoa New Zealand of the Black Panthers – one of the most influential movements in the history of black power in the United States. They sought to raise political consciousness and enthusiastically adopted the Black Panthers' Ten-Point Programme so as to teach Pacific families how to survive in New Zealand.

Collecting together interviews, memoirs, poetry, newspaper articles as well as critical analysis, *Polynesian Panthers* is an edgy, hard-hitting account of an important period in New Zealand's social and cultural evolution, and it provides the first account of the socio-political history of Pacific peoples in New Zealand.

Why it was important to produce a new edition

Since the first print of *Polynesian Panthers* in 2006, there have been developments at the local and international level. Locally, changes to the New Zealand school curriculum (NCEA Level 1 History curriculum) have generated a new interest in Pacific history. Over the last four years, a dedicated group of Panthers, Will 'Ilolahia, Tigilau

Ness, Alec Toleafoa and Melani Anae have been invited to South Auckland and inner-city secondary schools to give seminars about the Panther experience. Feedback by history teachers has been overwhelmingly positive.

Secondly, since its publication, two documentaries have been funded and produced – *The Dawn Raids*[1] and *The Polynesian Panthers*[2] which focused on issues which involved Panthers.

Thirdly, internationally – Black Panther Party artist Emory Douglas's invitation by the New Zealand Arts community has resulted in several visits to New Zealand, which has rekindled Black Panther Party links to the Polynesian Panthers.

Fourthly, a new generation of more politicised Pacific youth are now seeking new images and role models, new New Zealand-born-and-bred models.[3]

Current situation of the Panthers (as an organisation)

The PPP disbanded formally after the Springbok Tour. However, informally, 'once a Panther always a Panther' – the fundamental principles of the Party are promoted in whatever spheres Polynesian Panthers are involved in. These principles comprise the Panther platform of firstly to annihilate all forms of racism, secondly to celebrate mana Pasifika, and thirdly to teach the youth that the strongest form of protest is success, that is 'educate to liberate'. The Polynesian Panthers today continue to raise awareness of issues of social justice locally and globally in their own vocational spheres (religion, academia, arts, sport, music, professional occupations). As an organisation they continue to celebrate the anniversary of their formation June 16th 1971 and through music (Tigilau Ness), social reform (Will as a member of Waiata Trust and their 'affordable housing' scheme), and Melani Anae lecturing and inspiring a new generation of savvy young Pacific youth, the Panthers are inspiring a new Pacific generation to raise awareness of ongoing issues that impact Pacific peoples today – in their own environment, in their own context, in their own time, in their own place and in their own way. A very vivid example of this was when Anae's Pacific University of Auckland students played a vital role in the video project, *I, Too, Am Auckland*[4], a student-based initiative at the University of Auckland. This video explores experiences and perspectives provided by Māori and Pasifika students across a variety of academic disciplines, discussing their experiences with everyday colonialism and racism:

INTRODUCTION

March 24 2015 at 12:35am

Warm Pacific greetings! We have had the great pleasure of being inspired by the Polynesian Panther group who visited us last year at our university and gave us words of encouragement to pursue action to bring about our experiences of racism in our institution. As many would appreciate, getting to university is a massive achievement for many of our young Māori and Pasifika students and their families. However, once in, there are the 'unnecessary challenges' of having to deal with subtle racism regarding our place in university. With Targeted Admission Schemes and special academic success programmes – which have been advocated and fought for by groups like the Polynesian Panthers – there is now the stigma attached to Māori and Pacific students having these resources. So a small group of us mobilised and got working on the video project for the purposes of spreading the word out there on social media. This is the Auckland version, and so far the only New Zealand representation of a movement against the racism minorities face in … tertiary institutions. All three videos are on our YouTube channel.

Why it's important today for people to know the Panthers' story

From the feedback from students and teachers at secondary schools and the University of Auckland, we are seeing the birth of a new generation piecing together their own and our own history in this country, in their everyday life. They live in a world where the issues the Polynesian Panthers faced, such as racism, seem distant to their own reality and they often cannot believe this. But peel back the layers, and they are gradually realising that racism takes many forms, unlike the blatant racism experienced by Pacific peoples in Auckland in the 1970s, racism now is harder to seek out – institutional racism and discriminatory systemic forces across all social sectors are difficult to identify, yet their effects are there for all to see in the positioning of Pacific peoples at the bottom of all demographic indices.

Feedback credits the Panthers for being their vanguard, the real Pacific leaders of today in

New Zealand, and for raising these issues and putting them fairly and squarely in front of the power holders. The Polynesian Panther story is the story of Pacific in New Zealand and also the story of New Zealand becoming more and more aware of its real self. On one hand, the Polynesian Panthers helped shape the New Zealand-born Pacific identity in New Zealand, and on the other – in articulating Pacific issues – the activities of the Polynesian Panthers made New Zealand more aware of the multicultural fabric of its peoples and created a much more informed awareness of power differentials of ethnic minorities in New Zealand.

Polynesian Panthers is the first record of the Pacific rights and social activist movement in New Zealand, told by those who were there. Their actions were a desperate but necessary revolt against the entrenched stigma of racism and discrimination that Pacific Islanders faced trying to integrate into a New Zealand way of life during the 1970s and early 1980s, and today a strong impetus for a younger generation to 'Seize the Time'.[5]

ENDNOTES

[1] *Dawn Raids*. 5 June 2005, TV One. Auckland: Isola Productions.

[2] *Polynesian Panthers*, 2008. Auckland: Tumanako Productions.

[3] Transformations of pre-European role models, e.g., the Mau resistance movement in Samoa against the New Zealand Administration in Samoa; and the Nopele (Nobles) leadership in Tonga, which successfully resisted any form of European colonisation.

[4] The University of Auckland (2015) *I, Too, Am Auckland*. Auckland: Chillbox. https://www.youtube.com/watch?v=4iKLJTbN7uc

[5] Seale, B. (1970) *Seize the Time: The Story of the Black Panther Party and Huey P. Newton*. New York: Random House.

PART ONE

FROM FALEALILI TO PONSONBY

Following the Second World War, Pacific Islands' immigration to New Zealand increased, reaching a peak in the 1960s and early 1970s. New Zealand encouraged this trend as Pacific migrant workers provided a necessary pool of labour for its expanding industries. Yet by the late 1970s, the National Government was blaming Pacific peoples for overloaded social services and overstaying and portraying Pacific migration as a 'brown epidemic' (although such statements simply extended those of the Labour Government earlier in the decade). Politicians also constantly used the terms 'overstayer' and 'Islander' as if they were interchangeable. The combined effect of these representations of Pacific peoples was to create a stereotype of them as 'overstayers'. Few people at the time realised that Pacific peoples made up only a minority of immigrants to New Zealand. Also ignored or unappreciated was the reality that Pacific migrants did not represent a threat to New Zealand jobs, social services or the economy in general.

The theme of racism permeates the recollections of a generation of Pacific peoples and communities' from this time. One amusing account is of a rural New Zealander who considered Auckland to be where all the 'coconuts', 'Asians' and 'paper-pushers' live. Many Palagi from the South Island and rural areas had never met any Pacific people and could be incredibly ignorant, even asking, 'Do they still wear grass skirts and all that kind of thing?'[1]

The legacy of this stereotyping since the 1970s is that Pacific peoples are still subject to racist abuse by governments, media, and the New Zealand public in general. Pacific youth are still being called 'coconuts', 'black bastards' or 'bloody Islanders' in our streets, in our workplaces and in our schools.

Meeting racial prejudice

A GRAMMAR SCHOOL OLD BOY

I had a rocky time at [Grammar School] … I remember my first week at school, a guy came running up from the field one day and said, 'You know, they said no blacks can play.' I couldn't believe it … So we said, 'Who said that?' He said, 'Oh these big Palagi guys down there.' And so we went down there, grabbed the ball, and said, 'Who said that no blacks could play?' We were SO wild aye. And … pointed out this guy. So I've forgotten who went over … and boofed him in the face.

… But when I did my undergraduate degree I started critically reviewing what [that school] had done for me. I'm a loyal [school] old boy, but I have to say that that was the school that really opened my eyes on racism for the first time. Because when I was at [primary school], I was a valued PI member and I had a positive outlook on where I came from. The moment I got to [Grammar School] I was streamlined. Their expectation for PI students was really terrible. We got low-grade Pākehā teachers that were not really geared for working class ethnic children and it was also the first time I was called black bastard, in front of my teachers. So it was just sad. When I look back at my high school and I really enjoyed the sports and caught the racism on the other side of playing soccer …

That's why I'm so grateful to the Church for gathering our parents together and it gave us a sense of [being] important and special. And then suddenly you got out to a situation like at [Grammar School] where you thought some-body's saying otherwise! … and you sort of lashed out at them. But there were lots and lots of other incidents. Like in the end I got suspended … I was in the Headmaster's office three times. He asked me, 'Why? … You used to be such a good boy, and now you've turned into … a bad boy.' After, there was quite a big blow up … with the Polynesian kids. A Samoan was appointed head prefect … I don't think it was a token gesture, he deserved to be head prefect, but at the same time … They had to make some concessions for the fact that the school was no longer a white upper-middle-class school.[2]

A BOY CALLED BROKE: PART A – ARRIVAL FROM SAMOA
FA'AMOANA JOHN LUAFUTU

Ode To a Memory (Malaemalu by the Sea)

Evening meal is over
Now its Bible study at the Pastors
Who hit the Rock?
Who made the world?
Lets play screeching Bat
Come on lets catch the moon
On white sand we run to and fro
Hurricane lamps in the round houses
Begin to glow

Young ladies are at the spring
Vai puna a Tala cool as icewater
As old as Father time
Hair all washed and gleaming
Shampooed in Lemons & Lime
Combed thru in scented coconut oil
Under the moon to shine
In their lovers eyes
One by one the lights disappear
Spirits of the old people

Dance in ghostly cheer
Framed by shadows of Breadfruit trees
The ancient helmsman smiles in his sleep
His head on a wooden pillow
Snuggled up to my Grandmother
I hear stories of days gone by

Round houses all around me
As waves on the Reef
Crash and Die …

… And that night there was a family meeting. All my aunties and uncles were there. All of us children were told to catch the moon (*sapo le masina*) while the adults talked. During the meeting my father announced that he was taking his family to New Zealand … It seemed like the whole family was gathered at my uncle's place in Taufusi, heaps of umu for us to take on our trip, the house full of laughter and jokes. As it got closer to our going, I went outside for a shower and to get changed. There was a strange quiet in the family; it was time for a prayer. It was now the tears began to roll amongst the different brothers and sisters. I was sad and excited all at once.

I was dressed like never before, *ofu elei*, matching shorts and shirt and jandals (*pati pati*), my hair slicked down and my skin rubbed with sweet-smelling coconut oil which is made with *mosooi* flowers.

We made our way down to the jetty, some by car, some by truck. There were already families waiting there. I and some of my cousins ran onto the jetty. The tide was in, the water was a turquoise colour and clear; we could see a heap of different fishes swimming in and around beneath us. I could also see the *Tofua* out beyond the reef. Some families had already been ferried out and then it was our turn. My father called me up to embrace my family one more time, all my aunties and uncles, cousins, all crying. My grandfather and grandma requested us to write back and never to forget Poutasi or our family.

The *umu* and all our belongings were on the ferry. I had butterflies in my tummy as I hopped into the launch. We left the jetty. One of my aunties called out to my father, 'Ioane, don't forget to come back,' as we headed on out towards the *Tofua*. The launch pulled up beside the rope stairway beside the ship and we made our way up with all our stuff. The other families were sitting in groups on the deck sorting out their belongings.

Our family found a spot and we did the same. My mother breast-fed Eneliko. Losa and I ran off to the back. The boat was turning round and we wanted to see our family on the shore. They all looked like dots. We could see the clock tower and different shops, but the people were small. The *Tofua* pulled up anchor and set sail. Apia got smaller as we approached Manono and Apolima, and I marvelled at the sheer cliffs on one of those islands.

Then, it hit me – we were really leaving. I thought of all the different branches of my family. I thought of Taufusi, Faatoia, and all the villages in my area that I had been to for various reasons, that I could remember. From Sapunaoa to Siumu these were my thoughts, and as Apolima and Manono faded in the distance I thought of my mate Fili and our traps, our tins of herrings, our castor oil and the spring behind our school. And our circumcision. I relived the life I was leaving and a pictorial view came into focus. I saw Fili and myself, our pet dogs, our favourite haunts, our world in Poutasi, Nuusafee, Togitogiga Falls, the bridge, and the ancient paepae opposite the school, left hand

side of the road toward Satalo behind Poutasi. We'll be back, I thought. I asked my father later on. He was slow to reply: 'Someday,' he said, 'we'll return, someday.' It sounded doubtful, more like 'somehow'.

I first saw Auckland late in the afternoon, round tea time, just going on dark. The ground below was like a big chessboard, all divided and green with houses on it. Lights were starting to pop on in different areas of Auckland. Everything looked clean. This was the land of the Palagi. When my mother told me that they were houses, I wondered how we were going to fit into those funny things. The plane was landing, seat belts were tightened, my ears popped, we were on the ground. We stepped into a different climate, fresh and cold at Whenuapai Airport. There was a long bus ride to the bottom of Queen Street where we met my Uncle Gafa and Auntie Tusi. After saying goodbye to the others we hopped in a taxi and headed off to Grey Lynn.

On our arrival my Auntie Tusi told me to run to the door and pull the bell. I imagined the bell to be like the bells on the churches back home. No wonder I couldn't find it, besides it was really dark now and I couldn't see a thing. I waited for her. Inside, with tears of joy, my Auntie Ida and Auntie Mese greeted us. They were really happy. We all were. It had been a long trip, a long way to come.

The night we arrived there was another uncle who was a pastor. His name was Leua. My Auntie Tupulua and Uncle Sa, her husband, were also there to welcome us to New Zealand … We had a big feed, then the adults talked while we familiarised ourselves with the house – bathroom, toilet, taps in the house, wow!!! After a while we went off to sleep. Losa and Lilly slept with my aunties, I and my little brother in my mum's and dad's room.

Image from *The Islanders* booklet:
'Boy selling "The Star" newspaper.' Auckland: Shortland Publications, NZ Newspapers Ltd, 1976, p.1.

We arrived in Auckland in late October 1958, and God willing I was to start school in the new year. At that time there were nine of us in that house. My uncle and his wife, my two aunties Mese and Tusi, and the five of us. It was a full house. A lot of my family went through that house at various times. It was a springboard for many a wedding, seven in all, which my mum and dad organised. Our house was always full, all different members of our family, all working and living under the same roof.

The next morning my Auntie Mese took me to meet my cousins who lived at 17 Browning Street. My Auntie Tupulua and her husband Sa had eight kids in New Zealand. They had left behind two sons, Apelu and Tavita. The ones I met that day were Piko, Tapaau, Atenai, Puaa, Isaia and Lima.

Piko was working, Tapaau was at Auckland Girls' Grammar, Atenai and Puaa went to Grey Lynn primary, Isaia was not at school yet, and Lima was the same age as Eneliko, just a baby. The other two sons, Tone and Tavai, were already married and lived elsewhere.

We are related through our mothers. Tupulua's father was Lalau. He and my mother's mother were first cousins. Tatae was her name. Lalau's mother was Atina. Tatae's mother was Soloi. Soloi and Atina are sisters, hence our connection. My mother and Tupulua knew each other well as girls back in the village. Tupulua was raised in Lesalesatele and went to school there. Lalau would bring her to visit her family and cousins in Satalo. Lesalesatele was the adjoining village north of Satalo.

Tupula and Sa had left Samoa a couple of years before us. My cousins knew how to speak Samoan and we conversed frequently in our native tongue. It was they who helped me and showed me things in my formative years as a new arrival in New Zealand.

… [My cousin] and I are nearly the same age; he is the older by about four months. Atenai was a year older. We went everywhere together in those early years: to Grey Lynn Park, to the dump, to the movies at the Esquire picture theatre. I slowly got used to the place and really close to my two cousins. In the next few years these two would figure prominently in my life. Apparently they had stayed in Freemans Bay a few months before we arrived in New Zealand. Puaa and Nai attended Beresford Street Primary School in the street where they had lived, but had then shifted to 17 Browning Street. This was the Saifiti family, my cousins.

Between us, living in number 19, was an English family, Mr and Mrs Bush and their two sons John and Jimmy. Their house and garden were spotless.

Next to us on the right were a couple of flats. Right in front of our house was a street with a rise. At the top of the rise were the shops and a picture theatre, and it was here that the No. 3 Richmond Rd bus ended its round from town.

My Auntie Mese took me up to the shop and tried to get me to say 'One and a half loaves of bread.' Then she sent me into the shop. I fouled it up and my auntie came to the rescue and asked for the bread. Still eager to please my auntie, I said, 'Thank you please,' real timidly when the man handed over the bread. My auntie told everyone at home and they laughed, but at least I tried.

On Sundays we went to Church. It seemed that all Samoans at that time attended the PIC Church on the corner of Wellington and Pitt streets. We went there too with my Uncle Gafa and Aunty Ida. My cousins attended a different Church in Upper Queen Street opposite the Town Hall.

I had no idea yet of the language and was still fumbling things, but my cousins showed me around and I learnt slowly … I remember my first Christmas here in New Zealand very well. The bottom half of Browning Street was our playground, from Baildon Road down. Many a young cowboy met his fate here. On Christmas Eve the Sallies were out in force, brass bands on the back of trucks, other groups too, singing carols. 'Silent Night'. What a song! It was the first time I ever heard a choir sing that, live. Santa was out giving out lollies to everyone.

'And who's that man with the beard?' I heard my mother say out loud. My auntie explained, 'Se o Santa mea faa-atunuu palagi latou ia' (It's Santa one of those Palagi customs). 'Oh, I see.' 'La …' They all laughed.

Christmas Eve I was called in to get cleaned up. We were off to town. A week or two before my mother had written down something for me to recite. It was greetings in Samoan to family in Poutasi. It was to be broadcast live on the radio. I recited it to myself while I was getting ready. 'Do you know it?' asked my Auntie Tusi. 'Yeah,' I said. In our house we conversed in Samoan, not English. We were off to town, to the station. We met up with some of the people we had been on the boat with. Everyone was laughing and talking, remembering. Finally it was my turn and I was led into the room. There were a couple of palagi men there, saying something to my aunt. She told me I had to speak straight into the microphone. 'Right, now be good boy, don't forget your words'. 'One … two … now,' the man indicated with his hand. 'Talofa lava, o lou suafa o Faamoana Ioane Luafutu, E momoli atu ou alofaaga ia,' blah blah blah. Not one mistake. My auntie was proud of me. Afterwards I get a chocolate covered ice-cream, a Topsy, as we wait for the Westmere bus.

… I started school in the new year at St Joseph's Convent School. What a shock. I wanted to go to school with my cousins. I felt like a fish out of water. At that time I was given a Palagi name so as to make it easier for the teachers to say my name. It is John now. I went to school with one of my aunties to enrol my sister and me.

After talking to Mother Superior and signing all the necessary papers, I was shown my classroom. I still didn't savvy the Palagi language, and was totally lost in my new environment. My teacher was Mrs Collison, the only one that wasn't a nun. She was very nice and pleasant towards me and showed me my place to sit. I sat there in total ignorance. I was given a catechism and some other pamphlets. I felt totally out of place. Class resumed and Mrs Collison asked a question. Hands flew up. 'Mrs Collison, Mrs Collison'. My hand flew up too. 'Yes,' she says and points to me. I stand up and say, '*Fia Pi, Fia alu ile fale vao.*' All the kids laughed and Mrs Collison looked puzzled and came towards me. She turned around and went out the door. Soon she came back with two Samoan boys. They translated, she smiled and told them to take me outside. We talked and I found out their names, Don O'Dwyer and David Pereira. Their Samoan wasn't as fresh as mine. I was secretly proud of that, but at the same time felt a little inadequate. 'I'll teach them Samoan and they can teach me *Palagi*,' I thought to myself.

At [Grey Lynn School, where I transferred,] there was a swimming pool and each class had their turn at learning to swim. All of us Samoans knew how to swim already, and we'd race round the pool. Next to the school was a huge laundry and we could see steam coming from the different pipes and chimneys and smell detergent all round our school playground. Across the road from the laundry was the Weet-Bix factory. After school every day we'd all go to the factory door, and when there was no-one around we'd run in and pick up the Weet-Bix which had fallen off the conveyer belt which took them to the packers who were on the other side of the factory. There was always a group of us, mostly Samoans. Because of our lack of the vernacular, we developed our own kind of language and mannerisms which only the guys in our group could understand. A Palagi named Rodney and a Māori guy named Jockey were our constant companions in our Grey Lynn days.

On one side of our school was an old abandoned tennis court overgrown with bushes and trees. This was our playing area when school was over. We ate monkey apples, made huts and shot each other with shanghais. We'd do this every day after school. At times like this we were at our freest, back in Samoa, realising our affinity with the bush.

The following year Atenai and Faiaoga went on to Pasadena Intermediate, leaving Maresala, Simeti, Rodney, Puaa, John and Keith Hunter, Jock the Māori, as we used to call him, and myself at Grey Lynn. These guys were the ones we spent our time with after school. There was a closeness between us that went deeper than our just going to the same school. Our Palagi friend Rodney was well versed in Samoan language, but he could understand it better than he could speak it. The same with our friend Jock the Māori.

One Saturday Puaa took me to Maresala's place. They lived on Hakanoa Street. Their eldest brother, Faraima, played in a band with another Samoan guy named Dave Sheperd and we listened to them practising. Afterwards we would get out the gloves, choose partners, and go for it. The older boys were into bikes. It was here that I met two Tongan brothers, Charlie and Freddie White. Charlie was Faiaoga's mate, and his younger brother Fred was round the same age as Puaa and I. We became friends too. They lived in Francis Street off Richmond Road.

Long Barry, a Palagi mate of ours, was there also, and Robby Wells, a friend of the Simeti brothers, was another acquaintance and bosom buddy. After our boxing bouts we'd all truck off to Cox's Creek, the site of a rubbish dump. Here we would look for bike frames and parts. And we'd make rafts out of car roofs and sail out to sea till we saw the Auckland Harbour Bridge, then we'd go round the bend and swim and play round Herne Bay Beach. Sometimes when the tide was in, we'd stay and dive off the Cox's Creek Bridge, neat fun, and at dusk we'd head off home, raiding people's fruit trees. To us, this was all harmless fun.

… Some of the older boys started to go to the Speedway at Western Springs to watch cars, bikes and stock cars, and we followed in their footsteps every Saturday night. We younger ones watched proudly as our older brothers scrapped it out with local toughies. Peleve, Faiaoga and Charlie were all good scrappers, all class and combinations, but Atenai was in a class of his own, and he was a year younger than the other three. He had such a rage and indomitable spirit. He was like a bull even then. We all discussed their different styles and agreed that Atenai was a real *toa*. In the different scraps I saw, not one of our guys lost a fight in a one-out situation. I looked up to these fellows and was comfortable in my surroundings with them.

Atenai was in form one and Faiaoga and Charlie were in form two at Pasadena. Peleve was still at Richmond Road School with his brothers. I was in standard three, in Mrs Kestle's class. There were two Standard Three classes in our school and Puaa was in the other class with Mr Christianson. Tauvae was in my class. There was an Indian brother and sister, their last name was Patel. Mike the Niuean kid was there also. We were the only dark people in the class. The rest were all Palagi.

I befriended a Palagi boy by the name of Richard. He said that he would help me speak, write and read English properly. I accepted the offer, and took it to mean he would be my friend. We wrote messages to each other and gave them to the other pupils to pass along as we sat on opposite sides of the classroom. One day I drew a picture of him, as best I could, to make up for my lack of writing skills. I put his name on top, and wrote 'from John Luafutu' on the bottom, and sent it along in the usual way, folded up. I kept looking over to him feeling pleased with myself and hoping he was too. He got the letter, read it and wrote something to send back to me. Halfway across the room a girl peeked at the letter and started

laughing. The other pupils wanted to know what was in it too and there was a scraping of chairs as different ones got up to read my note from Richard. I got up to grab it also. I thought it was a joke and I wanted Tauvae to explain it to me. As I grabbed the letter Mrs Kestle walked in. She was annoyed with the class because we should have been sitting properly in our seats. She wanted to know what was in my hand. I tried to shove it in my pocket, but it was too late and she beckoned me to the front. After reading it, she indicated that she wanted me to read it aloud to the class. I tried: 'John Luafutu ees ahh.' She took the letter; 'Here, I'll help you,' she says, and with that she began, 'John Luafutu is a stupid bastard and a blithering idiot! Don't tell.'

Mrs Kestle was really mad about this and shouted, 'This is disgraceful. I want the person who wrote this to come to the front.' Everyone looked at Richard. He was grabbed by the ear and taken to the front by the teacher who pointed her finger at him and told him off. 'I don't usually do this, but Richard deserves this!' And she pulled a leather strap out of her drawer and gave Richard three on each hand. Richard grimaced and winced back to his desk.

Mrs Kestle hugged me and said, 'You poor, poor boy. Don't you believe any of this,' and she tore the letter to shreds and threw it in the bin. I was still lost about what was going on. At playtime Tauvae explained, 'It means you are *valea* and have no father,' she said to Puaa and me.

I was really livid about this and so was my cousin. We decided to wait for lunch before I would have a fight with him. Puaa was to be my backstop. 'You want fight, eh? C'mon, put up dukes, fair fight, eh.' He didn't want to know about it. Instead, he offered me his lunch. I looked at Puaa and looked at the lunch. 'OK.' We did this to Richard every day until one of the teachers saw us. 'Why?' he asked. 'He say I got no Fada,' I said. Puaa said nothing but just glared at him. The teacher went on, 'You've got no right whatsoever to do this. You're both just like Atenai. You're going to get six of the best each. I'll teach you to take people's lunch!'

We both had detention after school. Mrs Kestle, who knew what it was all about, would help me with Janet and John books and give me some of her leftover lunch, cake and fruit. I quite liked detention with Mrs Kestle. She was very helpful and kind to me. She would keep me in after school on purpose, just so I could catch up with my reading and writing. She was a great help and I looked to her as an adult friend, like an auntie. I was never afraid to ask her questions. I conversed with her in my freshly gained Samoan English and she would smile and correct my sentences and phrases.

On certain days we had school sports after lunch and the whole school would walk down to Grey Lynn Park. The fastest runners were Johnny Buchan, John Dearlove and Darryl Attwood. They were a year ahead of us and after they left for intermediate school it was down to Puaa and Rodney Elms.

We were now in Standard Four. At last Puaa and I were in the same class. Our teacher was Mr Webster who smoked continuously and had nicotine stained fingers and a deep booming voice. Puaa was really good at arithmetic but I was concentrating on how to read and write properly so most of the time I was given special assignments.

… One Saturday afternoon Auntie Tupulua sent Atenai and me to Manurewa to take our cousin Albert back home. He had been staying with them for a couple of weeks. It was a long bus ride out to where Albert stayed with his family. When we got there we walked to Albert's house where his

mother and sister Kiupi greeted us. We didn't stay long as we had to catch the returning bus to town. On the way to the bus stop we saw the bus pulling away. We started running but it was no good, we'd missed the bus and the next one wasn't due for an hour or so. There was a big queue of kids waiting outside the picture theatre for Saturday matinee.

We decided to spend our bus fare home on ice cream and cola. How were we going to get home? I said to Nai, 'We'll get a couple of those bikes.' We sat at the bus stop and waited till all the kids were inside. 'Which bike do you want?' says Nai. 'I'll have the blue one,' I said. When it was clear, Nai ran across the road and grabbed his bike and took off down the road. He stopped about a hundred yards away, and I ran across and grabbed the blue bike and ran to meet up with him. Not being a very good rider, I struggled with it all, but managed to keep up. We were both laughing as we rode towards the city.

After what seemed a long time we arrived at the old Mangere Bridge. We walked our bikes and peered over the bridge. The tide was out and I spotted something that looked like a gun in the water. It was a big rifle. I pointed it out to Nai and we went down to fetch it. Nai wrapped it up in his shirt and put it on the carrier of the bike and we went on, past Greenlane Hospital, the racecourse at Ellerslie, through Newmarket, up Khyber Pass Road to Upper Symonds Street, through Karangahape Road and down Ponsonby Road to Williamson Avenue, through Grey Lynn Park and home. We hid the bikes in the park and walked up Baildon Road to Browning Street. We hid the gun in the hedge. It was dark by now and the lights were coming on in the streets. It had taken us nearly four and a half hours to get home from Manurewa but at least we had a bike each. In the morning Nai, Puaa and I went down to get our bikes. We rode around laughing and carrying on. Nai said that Puaa and I could keep the bikes but he'd have the gun. That was okay by me.

Nai ended up selling the gun to a friend of ours, Philip, who lived up the road. However Phil's father informed the police. Now, in our area there was a constable, Mr Carson, who travelled around in a big brown Mercury V8. He came round to Nai and Puaa's place. We were all outside on the footpath playing around when he pulled up in his big car. He asked which one was Atenai, and talked with him and then with me concerning the rifle. I told him I had seen it first under the bridge, which confirmed Nai's story. He seemed satisfied and with a nod of his head he hopped back in his car. Tapaau came out to see what was going on. 'Oh nothing, the boys here found a gun, that's all, but if they find anything else like this please be sure they bring it to me,' he said. 'All right. Thank you Mr Carson.' He drove off. For a minute there our hearts had missed a beat. We'd thought he was going to ask about the bikes. Whew, that was lucky.

The next day after school we were approached by one of the older boys in our area. His name was Wayne and he wanted to buy both bikes for ten shillings because they were stolen. He told us to bring them to the park that night and he would give us the money. We went down to meet this guy and he gave us five bob, with the promise of a further five the next day. Next day we went down to the park for the rest of our money. We saw him but he refused to pay, saying there was nothing we could do about it. We told him that Nai was going to bash him up if he didn't pay up, but he said he didn't care who we told. So we went home really mad and told Nai what Wayne had said. 'Is that right?' said Nai, slamming his fist against the palm of his hand.

'We'll see him tomorrow night.' The next night Nai, Puaa, Rodney and I went down to the park to wait for Wayne. We took some sticks and rocks, just in case things didn't go our way. Nai was all hyped up, itching for a scrap. As it was, Wayne turned up with some story of the police finding the bikes, so we didn't push the issue. However, he didn't tell us that he had told the police everything, including whom he had got them from.

A couple of days later Mr Carson came round and charged Puaa and me with stealing bikes. We didn't let on about Nai, we just took the charges without saying anything to him. Puaa and I both got a good thrashing from our mothers at the same time. We rolled around on the floor screaming and yelling while our thighs were pinched, and we had welt marks all over our bodies from the coconut broom.

Auntie Tupulua, my mother, Puaa and I went on the No. 3 bus to the court. The Children's Court was right at the bottom of Queen Street, next to the Queen's Arcade, and we went up in the lift to the court. We were both put under welfare supervision for a year, under a Mr Stewart who was to come and visit us weekly at our homes. My mother and auntie were upset with both of us and tweaked our ears on the way home on the bus. 'What bad boys yous are,' they told us.

Toward the end of the year we were taken to Pasadena for familiarisation because that was where we would be going the following year. At Christmas break-up all the parents were called in for our prize-giving. Puaa got first prize for best at maths for our class and was given a certificate. I didn't expect anything but my name was called out. I got a certificate too, for 'Most Improved in English'. My mother was happy and proud of me. Puaa and I were both feeling good. 'Deeds not Words' was our school motto, and we felt that we had lived up to that somehow. We were sad too as this was the end of Grey Lynn Primary for us …

LOSA'S POEM:

Ode to Mum & Dad

My parents …
Eager to give their offspring
the best,
Moved to another land
'Aiga wooing them to
a paradise of money,
Better education & promises of
opportunity, without
the drudgery of sitting by the kerosene stove
doing the saka,
Life in New Zealand is
easy, they say …
Everyone has a fridge
and a TV
Freedom from the countless
fa'alavelave's
Why does my stomach
ache for Taro, Palusami
in a country where
you can have anything you want?
Why does my heart yearn
for, a view of our malae
in Poutasi.
Why do I feel like I don't
belong, in a country that I grew up in …
Why do I want to escape
all the time?
There's nowhere to run away to,
I've been sentenced to one thing

and there's a yearning to be
Somewhere else.
Dissatisfied, everything is tainted
by the feeling …
What is the feeling?
Not belonging, yet part of
Belonging but rejected
Some say I'm Fia – Palagi
Some say I'm Fia – Mauli
I've been remade & all
my parts don't slot together,
my parts slot in sometimes,
and pop out at the slightest
interference,
it doesn't have to be anything
Major!!
A word, a nod, an attitude
I am shattered
It takes a long time to be me again
As normal as I can be,
Under the circumstances.[3]

ENDNOTES

[1] Participant recollections in Anae, M. (1998) *Fofoaivaoese: Identity Journeys of New Zealand-born Samoans.* Unpublished PhD dissertation, Anthropology, University of Auckland.

[2] Participant recollections in Anae, M. (1998) *Fofoaivaoese: Identity Journeys of New Zealand-born Samoans.* Unpublished PhD dissertation, Anthropology, University of Auckland.

[3] Excerpt from Luafutu, Fa'amoana John (1994) *A Boy Called Broke: My Story, So Far.* Christchurch: Macmillan Brown Centre for Pacific Studies, University of Canterbury.

PART TWO
THE 'NEW ZEALAND-BORN' EXPERIENCE

Many among the first generations of New Zealand-born Pacific peoples – that is, the children and grandchildren of the first Pacific wave of migrants in the 1950s and 1960s – recall a sustained attack on their ethnicity as New Zealanders that has continued even beyond secondary school. They remember, too, their anger, frustration and confusion in response. Racist attacks on Pacific males tended to be more sustained and acute, and many males retaliated physically. Pacific females, in contrast, usually experienced more subtle discriminatory attacks. Their response was a form of passive resistance: they tended to internalise their feelings, remained silent and tried to be 'invisible'. However, some women are fervent in their declaration that they would not tolerate racist abuse against their children and would deal with racism in their own way.

In general, coping mechanisms for these earlier generations of New Zealand-borns during their teenage years involved anger and rage, a show of arrogance, and/or defiance bordering on confrontation. Some seemed to work through this stage at secondary school, but would revert to this 'angry' phase if they moved away from family and Church and into a milieu that rekindled feelings of inadequacy and confusion.

Another coping mechanism, common to New Zealand-borns in their response to racism and institutional racism was to become committed to social change. The typical trigger for this response was their own experiences of the bureaucracy, especially government departments, and perceived social injustices inflicted on themselves and families. Many gained these insights because, as teenagers, they accompanied their parents and grandparents to act as 'go-betweens' or 'interpreters' in formal interviews with government departments, school principals and other representatives of 'the system'. Thus, in their reactions against the system, some became involved in gangs or political movements and, as they grew older, channelled their energies into helping other Pacific peoples.

One further way of coping with racism or not being accepted as a New Zealander for some was to associate with tangata whenua.

Relationship with tangata whenua

The 'special' relationship with tangata whenua that many New Zealand-borns mention has never been examined or sufficiently explained before. In the period under discussion, from the 1950s to early 1970s, Māori as well as Pacific peoples were marginalised socially, economically, politically and educationally. The modern Maori renaissance had not yet begun in earnest; Pacific peoples were being tolerated by mainstream New Zealanders as the population was still not large enough to be seen as 'a problem'.

Many at inner-city schools recall being treated as one homogeneous group usually lumped under the label 'Polynesian'. Many joined the Polynesian club at school. Although the obvious reason was an interest in performing or taking part in Maori or Pacific culture, most Maori and New Zealand-borns gravitated towards the Polynesian club because it offered familiarity in the alien milieu of schooling in New Zealand, dominated by Palagi children and teachers, and the Palagi-orientated school curriculum. Sports groups were similarly organised. At universities, too, New Zealand-borns were drawn to Maori Studies and the only other discipline that dealt with familiar Pacific issues, anthropology. There was an ambiguity of ethnic boundaries between Maori and New Zealand-borns in schools and universities. In such ways Maori and New Zealand-borns learned together, played sports together, laughed together, and fiercely supported each other's political agendas. This close kinship was reflected in the way others saw them. New Zealand-borns recall being mistaken as Maori, mainly because they had the accent of a 'Kiwi' rather than a 'fob' or 'freshie'. Although many were caught in an embarrassing situation because of someone's assumption that they were Maori, a few New Zealand-borns chose to identify themselves as 'Maori from up north', mainly to avoid a lengthy discussion on why they did not have a freshie accent.

O a'u/I: My identity Journey

MELANI ANAE

Reading *Ola* by Albert Wendt (1991) made me reflect on my own personal life experiences. I concluded that some of Ola's experiences resembled mine.

Although I didn't feel alone anymore, I felt jealous of Ola. Ola was born in Samoa. I was envious that at least she was accepted by all and sundry that she is, was, and forever will be *Samoan*. She will always have her place in the sun. But my identity experience, and probably the identity experience of most New Zealand-born Samoans has been expressed as:

I am – a Samoan, but not a Samoan …
To my *'aiga* in Samoa, I am a *Papalagi*
I am – a New Zealander, but not a New Zealander …
To New Zealanders I am a 'bloody coconut', at worst, a 'Pacific Islander', at best
I am – to my Samoan parents, their child.

I can't even recall when I first felt this way. From birth and while growing up, I was warmly embraced in the cocoon of *'aiga* and Church. My parents had come to New Zealand in the early 1950s under the rhetoric of 'wanting a better life', or 'a better

Image from *The Islanders* booklet: 'Packed in to pay rent'. Auckland: Shortland Publications, NZ Newspapers Ltd, 1976, p. 9.

education for their children'. Perhaps this was the real reason. I'll never know (do I really need to know?). But for better or for worse out of a family of eight children, my youngest brother and I were the only New Zealand-born children.

The only world I knew was the *fa'aSamoa* that my parents brought with them (or that they could remember), and that was further moulded by our Pacific Islanders' Church (PIC). It found expression in obligations to family and *'aiga*, in *tautua* and *fa'aaloalo*, in taking care of grandparents and aunties, uncles and younger children, in discipline and respecting elders, in going to Sunday School and Church religiously and committing ourselves to Church activities, in accommodating visiting *'aiga* – often playing musical beds (be it on the floor or wherever else), in endless cooking and cups of tea, and in the many *fa'alavelave*.

My parents spoke English to us kids all the time; Samoan, their mother tongue, was reserved for speaking to each other and older members of the *'aiga*. This didn't even bother me at the time. We could all understand Samoan anyway. Although I remember Mum getting mad at me heaps for correcting her English …

School was a breeze, and I excelled at learning virtually anything – schoolwork, piano, in fact I became Dux and Head Prefect of my primary

Newton Pacific Islanders' Congregational Church (PICC) in the 1960s. This photo was taken from Edinburgh Street. The original, wooden Newton Congregational Church is on the left. This was taken over by PICC in 1949 and used as a church from 1949–1962 and as a hall from 1962–1979. In 1979, this building was demolished and replaced by a two-hall complex (Elisi and Fisher halls) at a cost of $600,000. The building on the right isthe 'new' concrete PICC, erected in 1962. From Anae, M. (1998). *Fofoaivaoese: Identity Journeys of New Zealand-born Samoans*. Unpublished PhD dissertation, Anthropology, University of Auckland, p.151.

school, at the same time! I was told it was a first. But I remember it only because my mother was so proud that she bought me my first ever wrist-watch to celebrate. What I tend to remember more were the school sores, the milk we had to drink before playtime and marching around the playground – military-style – in 'Houses' before starting classes day after day …

I was more than comfortable in these surroundings as a young child. This was the only world I knew, and wanted to know. I didn't see myself as Samoan, or New Zealander or 'different', or anything back then. Just a kid. But this soon changed.

I think the first stage of my becoming happened in 1963, when I was eleven. The wife of our Papalagi Minister took a group of us bright kids from Newton Church to the Town Hall to listen to the Youth Philharmonic Orchestra. I felt alienated. Why were we getting stared at? I felt estranged, but not completely knowing why. More importantly I was learning that I was 'different'. Although I was an avid music lover, and was the pianist for the youth choir, I didn't appreciate this particular musical experience.

Secondary school was the site where it all happened. I attended what was then an elite all-girls school. I was in the top-streamed class for the five years and soon became used to being the only Pacific Islander in class, though I hated it. Feelings of alienation and estrangement soon turned to anger and rage. Why wasn't the teacher picking me for answers? I felt invisible. I simply didn't fit in. Sometimes at lunchtimes I wanted to hide my lunch – big fat pieces of fresh bread with left-over *sapasui* or *pisupo*, just didn't seem to compare with the delicate, nutritious cheese and salad lunches of my classmates. In the same way,

where their girlish chatter focused around parties, boys, travel, concerts and fashion, my experiences of 'aiga and Church could only remain silently mine. I felt I had become mute. My participation in class was the same: rather than being vocal, I chose to compete with 'them' the only way I knew how – by getting As in exams and written work. I found solace in my friend Joan, a Maori girl from Ngapuhi, who introduced me to Maori issues. I felt a strong affinity to what Maori people were going through. I wondered why.

It was at this time also that I underwent a transition in my Church life and ideology. I began to question the givens I had been taught to accept. As I became educated, I became critical. I began to question the moral, spiritual and cultural 'rightness' of Western Christianity, especially how it had impacted on Pacific Island people. Why had Western Christianity replaced traditional religious beliefs so wholeheartedly? My growing disbelief in the existence of a God was fuelled by the tragic deaths of five members of my family: my sister, brother and 18-month-old nephew – killed in an aeroplane crash in Samoa, then my grandmother, my mother (struck down by incurable illnesses) – all in the same year!! (Was there a God?) How I even managed to pass the Bursary exam at the end of that tragic year I'll never know! I had spent half that year caring for my invalid mother and trying to cope with the loss of my family. I took passing the Bursary exam against all odds as a sign that this was the gift that God had given me – maybe I should try going to university. After all, that was what Mum would have wanted? But I had changed. I felt that Christianity was hypocritical – that there was a God for me was debatable. I became agnostic (is that the right word?). I drifted away from 'aiga, Church and Bible class.

"... girls all white and frilly ... boys in suits and ties ...", members of Newton Church Bible Class in the 1960s on the steps of the church. From Anae, M. (1998) *Fofoaivaoese: Identity Journeys of New Zealand-born Samoans.* Unpublished PhD dissertation, Anthropology, University of Auckland, p.150.

Many years later, I eventually reconciled my feelings about Christianity into a personal belief – I began a one-on-one relationship with God, and refused to believe that any denomination, religion or institution could mediate that relationship.

The next stage of my becoming was when I went to university. The empowering feeling that I experienced was awesome. The alienating nature of the university system wasn't a problem. I didn't care any more. I became political. I became involved with the foundation members of Maori activist groups and was part of their becoming. When the dawn raids and overstayers debacle impacted on our own *'aiga*, a few of us Samoans and Tongans (and others) got together and formed the Polynesian Panthers in Ponsonby ... a group which tried to alleviate the subordinate position of Pacific peoples in New Zealand – our parents, our grandparents, our *'aiga* [see Part Four] ... This was my 'romantic' stage, where I became bitter about being born in New Zealand, bitter about why inequality surrounded me, bitter about why my parents never *forced* me to speak Samoan. I wanted to reclaim my Samoan identity, and I romanticised about 'real' Samoan culture and life ...

I was a bit of a rebel in my younger days – especially after the plane crash and my mum died. I responded by doing 'naughty' things like wag school, meet up with boys. I remember one particular incident which changed my life forever regarding reclaiming my Samoan identity. I was wagging at a (boy)friend's house when my brother unexpectedly turned up (how he knew where I was, is still a mystery), told me off, dragged me home

Lupematasila Afaue Liliva Anae and Lucy Anae (nee Kelsall) and their children, 1954. From left to right: Annie, Lucy (carrying baby Edwin), Joseph, Everard, Lupematasila (carrying Melani) and Arthur (children absent: Lina and Jean). (Melani Anae personal archive).

and confronted my dad about the whole thing. I was so mad at my brother. The funny thing was that I knew he was right, the (boy)friend was a waster, I should have been at school. But the most important thing I learned was that my father and brother loved me enough to steer me in the right direction instead of the pathway I was on – the path to failure, confusion and self-destruction. On retrospection this was my first experience in the New Zealand context of *feagaiga* and it has guided me ever since in my relationships to siblings, *'aiga*, Church *ekalesia*, my own children and others.

The next stage was that I got a life … I married, but it didn't work out, mainly because he was a Maori trying to 'find himself' and in the process kept me from the things that made me who I was – my Samoan 'self' – in terms of my family,

obligations and Church. There was a separation and divorce but I was grateful that our union had produced a wonderful son, and had shown me that I could be independent and make my own decisions. I felt a power I had never previously known – that I could take control of my own life. Quite symbolic really since it was at this time in my life that I reclaimed my previous life as it were. I moved back to Ponsonby to be near my father and rest of my *'aiga*, I returned to Church (had I ever left?), and buried myself in full-time work, my studies and *'aiga*. All this was consolidated by a second union with a really neat guy who was secure in his own identity as a Maori (with Chinese ancestry also) and two more kids. Never in my life did I feel more secure about my identity than I did at this time.

Rev. Leuatea Sio ONZM, QSO, JP (middle) 1925–2005, with members of the Newton congregation. Migrated to NZ in 1950. Ordained Minister of PICC in 1957; retired in 1993. Affectionately called 'Uncle Bob' by PICC youth. From Anae, M. (1998) *Fofoaivaoese: Identity Journeys of New Zealand-born Samoans.* Unpublished PhD dissertation, Anthropology, University of Auckland, p.153.

I am who I am plus my husband, my son, my father, my *'aiga*, my other circumstances, and this sentence about who I am and the feeling I should be more …[1]

I now have a PhD in Anthropology, and teach at the University of Auckland … I've overcome the romantic stage. But now I am accused of being an 'academic', worse still, a 'colonised' Samoan.

The dilemma for me is trying to retain Samoan identity and *fa'aSamoa* values and epistemologies despite conflicting Western epistemologies and lifestyles. This is exacerbated by Pacific people who stereotype me as a Palagi academic and who, just because I have a PhD, think that I am not a 'real' Samoan. To me, the more pressing problem is how to not sacrifice my duties as daughter, sister, mother, wife, aunty, and member of Newton Church in the pursuit of *Papalagi* academic work which focuses on producing publications, undertaking research projects, teaching and speaking commitments, attending numerous overseas conferences, sitting on endless committees – things which take me away from my priorities of *'aiga* and Church, and my identity as a New Zealand-born. At university, my work is to redefine what counts as legitimate knowledge, and to expose the politics of research and the researched for Samoans, others and other Pacific Islanders. For my students, it is to be a good role model, to inspire them as I was inspired by a now eminent Fijian anthropologist,

Members of the Congregational Theological College, Auckland, in the 1960s. Rev. Lye Challis MBE, JP, BA (middle row, far right) 1903–1980, was the first Senior Minister of Newton PICC. Fondly remembered as 'Papa Challis'. From Anae, M. (1998) *Fofoaivaoese: Identity Journeys of New Zealand-born Samoans.* Unpublished PhD dissertation, Anthropology, University of Auckland, p.154.

who was my tutor in my undergraduate years. It is also to try and make space for my students, space for them and us to be who they and we are without having to continually justify their/our existence.

THE RETURN HOME

Another important stage of my becoming was my first trip to Samoa in 1994 … Although I had read extensively about Samoa, and had listened eagerly to other people's stories, nothing could prepare me for what I would experience. My most vivid recollection was arriving at 2 a.m. at Faleolo and the balmy drive from the airport to Apia …

I will never forget the sights, sounds and smell of Samoa that I experienced that night: seeing people in their open *fale* (houses) in the villages, sleeping, sitting or lying around talking, even at 2 a.m. … the leaning coconut trees creating welcoming silhouettes against the blue night sky; the smell of barbecued chicken as we drove through the streets of Apia. Words eluded me – was I 'home'?

I visited the Marist Brothers' School, where Dad said that as a boy he had thrown a bottle of ink at the teacher (Brother Francis), and my great grandmother Tosotagi's grave. It was here that I remembered my father's words about his grandmother Tosomaletagi whose mother, Sipa'u, had married Lima Pua'aefu of the great

Seumanutafa family of Apia, and how his mother Ane, had been betrothed to his father Sila from Falelatai to unite both Apia and Falelatai families and *gafa*. Standing there, I felt the strength and warmth of my ancestors' blood flowing through my veins …

[In Falelatai] I remember meeting all my *'aiga* – relatives who were strangers and yet had names of my brothers, sisters and other close relatives. I met a cousin who was named after me …

The next day, after the formalities of the welcome ceremony were over, the container of second-hand clothing my brothers and sisters in New Zealand had collected, together with hundreds of dollars worth of butter, sugar, rice, corned beef, flour, masi, lollies and onions, was broken open. It had been shipped to Samoa to coincide with our visit. The goodies were distributed to the eight different groups of our *'aiga* (in accordance with the *matai* titles of Dad and my eldest brother). Then too there was the large monetary gift.

Over the next few days various *malaga* visited us and money and gifts were exchanged. The village *komiki* put on various concerts for us with items they had composed and uniforms they had sewn especially for the occasion. It was a very mixed experience for me. My inability to communicate easily with members of my newly-found *'aiga* was frustrating. Although I could understand what they were saying, I could only respond in Samoan pidgin. Most of the time I said nothing, and I resented the fact that we had been put on some kind of pedestal. I did not feel superior to any of them, nor cleverer, I just admired them – their way of life, and regretted the comparatively poor living conditions and lack of much needed monetary resources to sustain a comfortable life, as we knew it.

It was this trip to Samoa which finally consolidated my identity, and which provided me with the secured identity of what being a New Zealand-born Samoan means for me.

Until this final experience, I had never owned my identity. Ever since I can remember, others have done and are still doing this for me. I, like my New Zealand-born cohorts, are continually being defined by others. They always will. But let them.

What I do know for sure is that for me, my identity journey has come full circle. It has been full of ownership of the choices I have made both good and bad, it is a reconciliation of challenges to my perceived self-identity as a New Zealand-born Samoan, even with the associated constraints and confusion caused by being called *Palagi* by my *'aiga* and elders, or bloody coconut by New Zealanders this entails. And this has been experienced with joy, pain, euphoria, blood, sweat and tears. But my identity is now secure. As a New Zealand-born Samoan I know my roles and responsibilities to my family, *'aiga* both in New Zealand and Samoa, and my Church in terms of *alofa, tautua, fa'aaloalo, feagaiga* and *usita'i* in the *va fealoafani* and *va tapuia*. As well as this, I know my roles and responsibilities in *Palagi* spaces in using my education, skills and knowledge to help other young Pacific peoples to motivate them to succeed.[2]

Stuck
ALEC TOLEAFOA

There were a lot of things happening in Ponsonby at that time – and in my own life. I know now in reflection that there was no way then, that I could possibly have coped with the tensions myself and others were experiencing. I did not have the emotional or analytical equipment through which to refract my experience. There were very few, if any, resources available to support Pacific people generally, let alone the rapidly growing phenomenon of New Zealand-born Pacific adolescents in particular. The traditional Pacific ways of resolving issues were not providing the liberating calm so desperately needed. Alcohol, drugs and involvement in crime provided temporary relief by masking the things I did not know how to resolve.

The education system provided little incentive or encouragement for Pacific students to do well. There was an expectation that most Pacific people would fail educationally and this was expressed at a narrow level, on numerous occasions by teachers instilling Pacific students with the notion that our destiny resided in the rank and file of unskilled labour. At a broader level, school zoning denied most of us access to schools with high achievement rates. The majority of students from migrant families in inner-city Auckland could only enrol at a particular school, which specialised in technical skills training.

My first attempt at School Certificate was run through with a sense of inevitable failure, due in part to an unsympathetic education system and in part to frequent absences for court appearances and probation issues. Other absences related to the problem of reintegrating to the relative innocence of school life, and just being a 15-year-old having experienced the realities of society's underbelly and living with its stigmata.

A second attempt at School Certificate was a rerun of the first. This time though, I was in court for a serious assault charge, which had the likelihood of escalating to manslaughter. I managed to evade arrest for a time until one morning the police discovered me at my family home and placed me in custody.

In the cells, I thought about my future, which included preparing for a prison term. Perhaps for the first time I felt stuck. Stuck in the slums of Ponsonby, stuck within a stereotype, stuck in and between two cultures, stuck with a destiny divined by demographics, and of course, stuck in custody.

Around this time, I had drifted onto the periphery of what was to become a turning point and an enduring relief from the sense of being stuck. Here were people my own age who, in a focused, sustained and engaging way, challenged the structures and myths which were effectively keeping Pacific people and other minorities stuck on the margins. For example, the myth my teachers had instilled – that we were only good enough to join the long lines of process workers – was a farce. There were other options and aspirations open to me and to us, after all.

The Panther experience provided the analytical tools needed to articulate what were otherwise homeless thoughts and emotions, urgently needing a context. I was able to distil some clarity from a tangle of confused thoughts. The high-risk behaviours I engaged in, were explicable within the broader contexts of social justice, racial discrimination and bicultural schizophrenia.

The influence of the Panthers awakened the understanding and realisation that Pacific people in New Zealand live in, and often collided with, a political and cultural regime that had no concern for our well-being. The only people concerned about improving race relations, access to better housing, educational and employment opportunities, was us ourselves. As a Panther, I was actively participating in the solution.

Memories of a first-born New Zealand-born

'THE SHILLOUETTE'

The first time I used the word racial discrimination at Mt Albert Grammar School (MAGS), the teacher asked if I knew what it meant. Demographics weren't even part of my vocabulary then. My attempt to shock and impress the teacher with a new word only left me feeling embarrassed. I don't think I really understood the concept whether subtle or obvious at that time. I never experienced deliberate and direct discrimination in a way that I could have understood or comprehended. But that experience in the classroom left me feeling uncomfortable and inadequate, not being able to articulate my thoughts.

Anyway, who gave a fuck about what some Palagi English teacher was trying to do in advancing our place in society. I had always been told throughout my school years, since primary school, that we would not amount to anything other than manual labourers.

The only other discrimination I ever felt was being at the Fonoti's place. They were one of the first Samoan families that owned a TV in Summer St. It was humiliating watching TV at their place. Feeling like second-class neighbours because we didn't have a TV. We stopped going to their place to watch TV after I complained to my mother. I couldn't put up any more with the acidic murmurs from the juniors in the household.

There never seemed to be any peace for me, in my recollection of the period 1962–1973. Myself … within and the world, globally without, the Vietnam War; Student Protests, Kent State, assassinations of the Kennedy Brothers, Martin Luther King, Malcolm X, television … rock 'n' roll. And if you walked down the Ponsonby Road footpaths in bare feet, the fine, grey, black dust left a dark film on the soles of your feet. Especially around the Three Lamps area and places where heavy social PI traffic congregated to buy, talk, bet and drink. Busy human activity voices, interaction … Relief from their daily drudgery, regaining their dignity for the weekend … Big smiles: the chorus of sounds and rhythms of Island languages.

And the big heaps of violence in the home … all quite normal, everyday tinderbox situations. And of course, the constant reminder that nuclear annihilation could happen at any moment.

I recall as a young child having the frightening task of having to peek behind the main public bar doors of the Gluepot in search of dad. Being the eldest born in New Zealand, this was not one of those missions that I could say I would handle with zeal. Just pushing those twin-panel doors slightly ajar and to hear the drone of alcoholic voices rush out, sounded like a well-worn vinyl record stuck in its groove. And that peculiar rancid smell of spilt piss and the thick tobacco fumes; for a second in all of eternity the world seemed to stand still. Whoever was in sight of those swinging doors, looked through eyes of red … Look at the child at the door … It was all too fleeting and revolting for a child … I first became aware of my surroundings and my environment as a child in Summer Street, Ponsonby, during the early sixties … St John's Methodist Church in Ponsonby was our family Church although I was baptized at the PICC in Newton … Going to Church never provided me with the spiritual comfort that I instinctively craved. However, the scriptures were great stories and when I applied myself and managed to attain credible results in scripture exams. But the favourable results were more to do with the incentive to avoid the Samoan pinch on the inner thigh which the Sunday school teachers expertly applied with casual sadism.

One day, Tigi Ness and his family moved into the street back in the 1960s. They were a mysterious family who kept to themselves. For many years I would observe Tigi, his mother and sisters coming and going from his house in a quite dignified manner. Theirs was an almost serene and focused simplicity tempered with the mundane chores and errands for their whanau. Many, many moons later through a cousin of mine, Henry Tuiavati, I was fortunate to know Tigi at MAGS where our paths crossed and we remain friends to this day. Tigi was an A-stream student. For a lot of the boys from the hood then, Tigi's place was a place of refuge; somewhere to regather our solidarity in the hood; talk, eat and share the wonderful receiving openness of the Ness family. [For more on Tigi's story see Part Four.]

One day at MAGS I looked around and I realized that all those peers that I attended school with and considered friends were no longer in my class; they had left school. Some like George Pouesi had actually gone out and gotten jobs and girlfriends. So I dropped out and just hung out at the Paramount Billiards & Snooker room in Queen Street; sometimes sleeping downtown in the Britomart carpark on the odd night. Man was that a cold fucking experience. I remember shrinking and shivering my balls off in the stairwell. This street life was a fucking drag.

My mates, Gordon Stanley and Gus Guttenbeil, would turn up now and then at the billiards room. This place that had a lot of bravado: pool sharks and wannabes. Another smoked-filled joint tinged with the smell of old leather from the long chairs that lined the walls. It was home to us during the long days in this pool hall; waiting for something to happen.

Everyone was taking time out from their families till the inevitable day of reckoning when concerned parents and guardians would come down those steps to collect their children. Mrs Stanley tracked Gordon to the pool hall and came to collect him. I felt that Mrs Stanley held me responsible for her son's decision-making processes. Shit the 'fucker' turning up one day and shit, why am I to blame? Gordon was able to get his life back on track; quickly relocating to another school. Not long after that day Mr Guttenbeil came to collect his nephew and promptly put him back on a plane to Tonga. I felt an emptiness as I watched my mates end their adventures and return home to their families …

Eventually I ended up in Mt Eden Prison where I used the alias Paul Reid. It was a name of a Palagi boy at Richmond Road Primary School. In my boyhood days I had mentioned to Sven Guttenbeil that I would some day use the name. Fortunately for me he remembered it, and used it as a hunch for my mother who was desperately looking for me. She tracked me down under that name …

ENDNOTES

[1] Wendt, A. (1991) *Ola*. Auckland: Penguin.

[2] Excerpt, with minor editing, from Anae, M. (2003) 'O a'u/I: My Identity Journey'. In Fairbairn Dunlop, P. and Makisi, G. (Eds) *Making Our Place: Growing up PI in New Zealand*. Palmerston North: Dunmore Press.

PART THREE

PONSONBY – THE 'LITTLE POLYNESIA IN NEW ZEALAND' – AND THE GANG EXPERIENCE

The situation for Pacific Islanders in New Zealand, and especially in Auckland, changed in the 1970s. Wider events had an impact: with the first oil crisis in 1973 and the loss of New Zealand's major export market after the United Kingdom entered the European Economic Community, unemployment began to rise. People began to see Pacific peoples as a threat for three reasons. First was the false perception that they were taking New Zealanders' jobs away from them. Secondly, the media took a stance of populist racism, portraying Pacific peoples as a 'big problem'. Thirdly, there was a misconception that they were violent, rapists, criminals of the most vicious kind. So in 1974, on the initiative of Prime Minister Norman Kirk, the government focused on Samoans and Tongans, who did not have rights of free entry to New Zealand like Niueans, Tokelauans and Cook Islanders. Police and immigration authorities took decisive action against overstayers. After a lull, the lead up to the 1975 election brought a further vicious and widespread campaign against Pacific peoples. The overstaying campaign became a hallmark of the 1970s.

In contrast to the 1980s, when the emphasis shifted to controlling numbers, immigration policy in the 1970s was overtly racist. Even cabinet ministers were outright racist towards Pacific Islanders. Even though there were far more overstayers from the United Kingdom and the United States, Pacific Islanders were targeted because they were no longer needed. Even some who were not overstayers were targeted. Civil rights had reached a low point.

Such overt racism gave rise to suffering, rage, anger, humiliation and shame for many Pacific Islanders. Their view of the police, who acted on behalf of the politicians, changed immeasurably.

One way that Pacific youth sought to cope with these circumstances was to join gangs. In doing this, the underbelly of violence, drugs and crime in the inner city took on new and urgent dimensions. While other Pacific people were going to Church, buying villas in Ponsonby (the 'little Polynesia of New Zealand') and shopping on Karangahape Road, rival gangs fought for patches and territorial supremacy. Parts of the city were carved out and fiercely defended from interlopers.

Being a Polynesian

Thinking of New Zealand as a paradise of work and money.
Eating corned beef, taro and tinned fish.
Having only one bed for three people and sometimes no bed, just the floor.
Saying kia ora, kia orana, talofa, fakalofa lahi atu, ni sa bula and malo e lelei to everyone you see.
Sending bad children back to the Islands so they won't get into any more trouble.
Pinching from the rich and selling to the poor at half price.
Being good-looking and chasing all the girls in sight.
Being scared when a man in a suit visits the house.
Having an argument and letting the whole street hear about it.
Being called a coconut and pretending to be happy about it.
Being called an overstayer in our own part of the world.
Being hassled by the Police when walking alone at night.

Working in a factory to be with one's mates.
Being communist long before Karl Marx.
Being bilingual.
Having your name mispronounced by people
who don't care or won't try.
Having untold fathers, mothers, uncles,
aunties, cousins and relatives.
Being exploited as a cheap labour force by
the government.
Welcoming a lavalava in the middle of a
crowd.
Wearing only a tee shirt and pretending not to
be cold.
Knowing that somewhere out there in the
Pacific is a place called 'home' when racism
gets too heavy.
Being a Polynesian is hard, being a Polynesian
is to laugh, being a Polynesian is to cry, being
a Polynesian is forever.[1]

Remembering the Ponsonby end of Karangahape Road

MELANI ANAE

Karangahape Road connects Ponsonby Road to Auckland's main street, Queen Street, but the tell-tale signs of old, decaying buildings, billboards of half-nude females and reclining ladies of the night stretched above entrances to strip bars and sex shops indicate that this part of K'Rd is Auckland's sleazy red-light district … K'Rd is also known for its sea of blue-uniformed Auckland Girls' Grammar School girls who flood into it, in and out of the yellow buses every morning during the week at 8 a.m. and 3.30 p.m. every afternoon. There is a third group of people who frequent and who are seen often along this street during the week. This group is more distinctive in the weekends, especially on Sundays – middle-aged and old women who most often wear white and hats, younger and elderly men in suits and ties, boys in Nike sports shoes and gear, some young women and girls abreast of trendy fashions, others in *puletasi* or *pea* (lit. 'pair'; woman's two piece costume-neck to ankle-length). This group are the *ekalesia* of Newton Pacific Islanders Church which is in Edinburgh St, a street which branches off K'Rd, between the Pleasure Chest and the Pink Pussycat.

In the old days this part of K'Rd also consisted of a few shops – a dairy, a fish 'n' chip shop, some second-hand clothing stores, a shoe-repair shop, a bakery, a doll-hospital. Now these have given way to a trendy mall, shop owners are loathe to lease, on the top of which used to be one of Auckland's new landmarks, the 360-degree revolving restaurant. As a child I remember having fish 'n' chips for tea almost every night because of all the choir practices, meetings and workshops we used to have at Church every day of the week after school. I also remember walking home, or often waiting for my bus at the bus-stop just outside the Pink Pussycat on Sundays. Oblivious to what the strip clubs represented I never ever stopped to think of what I must have looked like – a young Samoan girl in frilly dress and shiny black shoes juxtaposed against a backdrop of a white, seductively beckoning nude temptress. wondered why the headmistress of the Grammar school forbade us to wait for our bus at that bus-stop in our school uniforms! … K'Rd, despite its

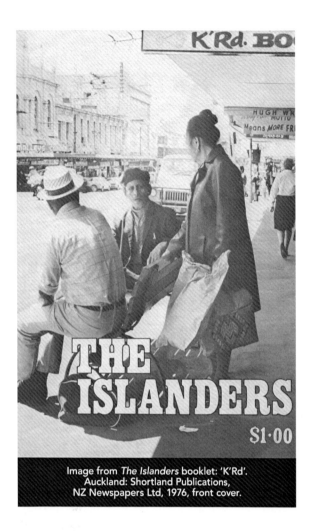

Image from *The Islanders* booklet: 'K'Rd'.
Auckland: Shortland Publications,
NZ Newspapers Ltd, 1976, front cover.

questionable reputation, used to be regarded as a mecca by Pacific peoples in the 60s, 70s and 80s and it is not difficult to understand why. The suburbs of inner city Auckland, Grey Lynn, Ponsonby, Herne Bay were colonised by Pacific peoples, viz. Samoans, Cook Islanders and Niueans way before the trendy-yuppie-apartment-café people-culture that pervades this area today. Why? Because it represented the site of the first Pacific ethnic Church in New Zealand – Newton Church – which became a magnet to all Pacific new arrivals to New Zealand; it became a gathering place for Pacific peoples throughout

Auckland – before they shifted and 'were shunted' out to the outer suburbs of Mangere, Otara in the south and Henderson and Te Atatu out west, and Glen Innes in the east, and Beachhaven/Birkdale on the North Shore. K'Rd used to be 'the place to be' especially on a Thursday late shopping night where hordes of Pacific young people and elders used to ascend, to shop, talk, meet, eat, hang out with mates.[2]

A boy called broke: Part B – journey to the cells

FA'AMOANA JOHN LUAFUTU

One day after school, we were playing around inside an empty building on the edge of the camp and by chance we came across an opossum up on the rafters. 'Watch out man, those things can scratch your eyes out,' says Maresala. I'd never seen an opossum before. Puaa and I climbed to the rafters trying to get a better look at the animal. We'd backed it into a corner and decided to smoke it out so that we could give chase. However the rafters caught alight and were burning. We tried to put it out but to no avail. All our other mates were telling us to leave it. The possum screeched and leapt off the rafters and out of a window, but the fire had started to spread underneath the roof of tar-pitch material.

We took off after our mates. At the top of the pines beside the stadium fence we caught up with the rest of the boys. 'Ooh, yous are in the shit,' they said to Puaa and me. We watched from the top of the hill as the flames hungrily devoured the building. We heard the wailing of fire engines as we walked down Francis Street towards Richmond Road.

Next morning at assembly, in front of the whole school, John Luafutu and Puaa Saifiti were asked to come forward. We broke off from our class lines and went to the front of the assembly. We saw our mates in amongst all the pupils of our school. They had knowing looks in their eyes. To this day I don't know how they got to single Puaa and me out, but single us out they did.

On entering the principal's office we were met by two detectives who took us to Auckland police station, where the university is now. It was a big brick building, cold and damp. Here we were told to make a statement and then charged with arson. We were careful not to implicate any of our mates. We took it on ourselves to shoulder the blame for it all. The coppers took us back to school. It was lunch-time.

The following week found us at the bottom of Queen Street in the Children's Court dressed in our school uniforms. There were other kids in court. We were the only Samoans present.

Mr Stewart, our probation officer, was there and he tried communicating with our mothers in broken English. He had recommended in his report that Puaa go to the boys' home for eight months. I was to have weekly supervision with him every Tuesday evening for twelve months, with the warning that we'd both be made state wards if we didn't behave. His recommendations were accepted by the judge. I left the court without my cousin. It was a tearful farewell as we waited for the court officer to come and take Puaa away. Our mothers were crying. 'Ia Puaa, tama lelei ile na mea lea ave ai oe.' We were all crying. My auntie, mother and I catch the No. 3 bus for home without Puaa.

… [After Puaa came back from Owairaka,] Puaa and I were starting to wag school more than the other guys and our last year at Pasadena passed by real fast. We still attended 'clubs' with most of our mates but some of the older boys started to go down to the Queen's Arcade at the bottom of Queen Street to play snooker on Friday nights. Gradually we started following them down to the snooker rooms. It just seemed like the thing to do, following our older bros even though some of them had finished school. We were in Form Four then. Seddon High was full of Polynesian pupils of all kinds, Tongans, Niueans, Maoris and Rarotongan girls and boys …

Behind Tattersfield's mattress factory was a big dump called Cox's Creek. Here we'd make rafts out of car roofs and sail under the bridge out to sea. This was a regular Sunday afternoon event. Early evening found us raiding peaches and apples off people in the area. We looked upon this as a bit of a lark with nothing really wrong about it, just harmless fun.

Later we progressed to the factories, warehouses and shops round the area. It was mostly Puaa and I. It wasn't long before we were involved with the law again. It was becoming quite frequent, wagging school, breaking and entering, with me leading, so that I eventually took off from home rather than face my old man, whom I knew would be boiling mad if he was to find out all this about me. It was a good time to run away. The carnival had arrived in town and was happening at Western Springs.

In the bush surrounding the lake, I and a couple of friends made a hut which was where I hid out for about a week, about as long as the carnival lasted. The police found me one Sunday and took me back home. I told them why I shot through.

They told me that my parents were really worried about me. When I got home my mum was crying. After she'd talked to me I had a bath and a feed, feeling somewhat relieved that I never got the broom.

So it was back to school, more wagging, night-time raids, petty thieving and suchlike. My dad would play detective and follow us sometimes but we usually gave him the slip.

There would be quite a few of us walking to school together, a cloud of smoke from our cigarettes as we walked along, littering the footpath with biscuit and cake wrappings which we'd pinched from the shops.

One of our Niuean mates we used to call 'Monkey Man' was late one morning and had to run to catch up to us. When he caught up he said, 'Gee you guys look like a bunch of Niggs walking along together,' and so from a simple comment like that the name of the 'Niggs' was born. We took that name on with much pride for a long time, with Baba at the helm, our acknowledged and popular leader. More people identified with us as we went on. It was a real mix of races, Palagi, Maori and Pacific Islanders – a real cultural mix.

A few of us were leaning more and more towards the snooker rooms in town, catching the last bus home, No. 3. Most of us either lived in Ponsonby or Grey Lynn and the Richmond Road bus served us well. Sometimes we'd walk home by way of Ivan's Place, a restaurant on the corner of Anglesea Street and Ponsonby Road, for fish and chips. Sometimes Puaa and I would go to the Picasso, a night club on Grey's Avenue to see Piko and Nai who were knocking round with some other Samoan guys of their age group, along with three of Baba's brothers, Squash, Falaimo and Faiaoga. Here I first saw a guy called 'Tex' who seemed to

be the one they focused on. I was to meet him later. Also I met Joe Scanlan.

These guys were the original King Cobras, a real hard crew with which we identified because of close ties. As far as burling and heart went, the KCs of this era were never to be surpassed. Their principles were high – no narking, no running to police, everything settled on the street level. I witnessed a lot of deportations as a result of some of the things that went down. Some good 'blues' happened at the Picasso. Watching some of these fights was a source of pride for me and I looked up to these guys, mostly because they were Samoan – like me.

Not long after this about five of us ran away from home. We stayed in the bush down at the bottom of Hakanoa Street so it wasn't really running away at all. We saw our mates every day, and were doing 'burgs' at night. It seemed a long time, but really was only about two weeks before the wheels fell off, and we were hauled before the court again with a long list of charges to face, petty thieving mostly.

Puaa and I were soon in Owairaka Boys' Home. It was the first time for me. I was in cubicles and Puaa in security. I met different guys and learnt why some of them came in, burgs, car conversions, theft, runaways, anti-social behaviour, they were all here. We all had duties, mostly scrubbing, cleaning and lots of PT. Everyone had to run around the footy field every morning several times, before going to the dining room for a cup of coffee or cocoa. Then it was cleaning duty before breakfast. Afterwards it was get ready for school or work parties. I was put in the garden party. No school …

We were there for about ten months but had no idea what was happening with us … One day the housemaster said we'd be going to Levin, he didn't know how long for. I felt sad for my family knowing how worried they'd be, but at the same time I was excited as hell. Levin seemed a long way away. I hadn't been out of Auckland before except for a Boys' Brigade camp. This camp was a different can of beans, but I still harboured a sense of adventure about the whole thing. It was all about discovering and the excitement of the unknown …

Kohitere [Levin Boys' Training Centre] was a big complex with its own dairy, woodwork shop, engineering, school, garden and forestry division. There was a heap of different blokes there, mainly Maoris. Puaa and I both ended up in a forestry

gang … After a few months, all was going pretty. I got into guitar-playing and sports and made friends with some of the guys.

Some of these friendships carried on outside Kohitere once I was released. Most of the guys I met there in 1965 I was to meet again, in borstals and prisons, throughout the New Zealand penal system.

Kohitere to me was a contradiction, in that while it was good to meet and make new friends, I also got to know a whole lot of negative things. I suppose these kinds of places are set up for those that want to help themselves, but for me it was just confusion. I really did not know myself so as to

Image from *The Islanders* booklet: 'K'Rd, Barker and Pollock'. Auckland: Shortland Publications, NZ Newspapers Ltd, 1976, p.11.

Images from *The Islanders* booklet. Auckland: Shortland Publications, NZ Newspapers Ltd, 1976, p.44.

help myself. The place had no function to meet the needs of a Samoan like me or my cousin still we're gonna go with the flow.

I was here for twenty odd months but it seemed like years. I escaped towards the end because I just couldn't hack it. I ended up in the secure block which had just been built. It was real hard, running on double time everywhere. Smashing concrete foundations all day with sledge hammers was our job. It was real discipline stuff. We weren't allowed to talk to each other. There were about six of us in there. Most were Palagi. I was the only Samoan. For some reason I was proud of that fact …

Some nights I would lie on my bunk and visualise where I came from. Poutasi and Samoa seemed far away and getting fainter day by day. On nights like these I'd feel real sad thinking of my father and, my sisters and brothers and my whole extended family. I'd say to myself:

What am I doing here?

What am I going to do when I get out?

Is it because I'm just bad or is it fate?

Sometimes I'd be angry at God or whoever it was that made this world. I had no idea of what I was gonna do once I got out. Of the time I spent here the only good thing I learned was how to plant trees and scrub cutting, but I did learn everything negative like burglary, shoplifting, drinking booze, home-brewing, armed robbery, safe cracking, tattooing and rebel, rebel. And a hatred for authority, arising from house masters in Owairaka, going on to screws in prisons.

When I think of Satalo and Poutasi and Falealili [the village where I was born] and my present situation I realise sadly that I'll never be the same again. Somewhere between Fa'amoana and John there was a break-down (*Gau*) of sorts which had a devastating effect, leaving me here staring at the concrete ceiling of my cell.

I hadn't seen my cousin Puaa for a few weeks. I suppose he'd gone through a few changes himself. It's hard to decipher at which point one culture overtakes another – or is it a slow, subtle process, with the individual struggling to retain whatever it is that made him or her that special being in their own right?

Image from *The Islanders* booklet: 'Factory workers having lunch'. Auckland: Shortland Publications, NZ Newspapers Ltd, 1976, p.13.

I just wanted out because Kohitere for me was like a primary school for criminals. I ended up with the attitude that if I got to borstal, I might see some of my new buddies that I made while in here. And take another step up to being a fully fledged hood, whatever that meant. I was in the secure block for three months after which I was allowed to go back with the rest of the institution.

Puaa and I came out to a new currency. New Zealand was changing the pound to the dollar. I likened that to Puaa and me. We were changed too, in many ways; bright and shiny like new fifty cent pieces. We came out to a rapidly changing Auckland in the sixties, to try out all the things we'd learnt at Kohitere, Levin. The fruition of this

brought us a lot of pain as well as years in the different institutions and jails in New Zealand. The stigma of this we'll carry to our graves.[3]

Foof's story

I started getting into blues music, picking up my licks in the different houses, borstals and jails where I ended up along the way. Part of that history is connected to the fact of being an ex-gang member in the Niggs and Black Panthers in Grey Lynn/Ponsonby in the early 60s.

A soldier-member amongst many, under Tex, an original member of the first Polynesian gang in Ponsonby under the name of King Cobras, which our older bros and cousins all belonged to at some time or another. But this is a different time and many other gangs were sprouting up on what we termed our turf!

This is but a peek into how things tie up, but is by no means the whole picture.

In the bar where the students drank, it is buzzing as is usual on a Friday night. A group of students get drinking around a table: they were all present at the last lecture of the day concerning the race issues of the American Negroes.

Willo, a Tongan student, sits drinking with some of his classmates. They are all first-year grads, most of them Palagis from various backgrounds. None of them has any idea that their Tongan colleague is a hard-core member of the Black Panthers Gang from Grey Lynn/Ponsonby that represents a wide cross-section of the population. Willo lives with a family in Lincoln Street, connecting Ponsonby Road to Richmond Road.

Willo sits quietly sipping his beer, listening to the discussion going around the table. It is about the Black Panther movement in the States. Willo thinks about his own gang: 'Wouldn't it be great to get all his gang bros to think political. After all, there are parallels to our own people in Aotearoa with what's happening Stateside. Hmm …' he wonders. Picking up his bag, Willo checks inside to find a copy of *Seize the Time*. 'Good, I'll take this to show the boys later,' thinks Willo to himself.

Willo is the only one of the Black Panthers to make it through to tertiary education. All the rest dropped out of school early: some are in prison; some are at sea. Some are not working but into crime; some have been deported to their islands of origin. He feels quite lucky that he's come so far and thankful to his Panther Brothers for making sure he got away from the cops during the many gang confrontations that went down.

Only a week before, the Wehrmacht from South Auckland (mostly Maori fellas) came to town for the first 'Battle of the Bands' ever held in Auckland at the YMCA. The Wehrmacht were gathering around the front. Suddenly from the side, Willo, Wulf and Rock attacked head-on, while across the street came Moose, Flamo and others, running with fence palings to sandwich the Wehrmacht. They were panicking and starting to scatter. The Panthers came away with minor injuries but the Wehrmacht fled leaving a couple out cold in Vincent Street. They got bashed and their heads jumped on, till the police got there. The Panthers chased the Wehrmacht all the way to Khyber Pass Road, avoiding the cops who were all over the streets around the K Road area.

This is the scenario in Willo's mind's eye as one of his fellow students calls him: 'Willo! Your shot.'

'Nah, you play! I gotta make a phone call.' Willo makes for where the phone is. Dialing a number Willo waits, 'Is any of the bros there?'

'Yeah … Who wants to know?'

'This is Willo. Are any of the Panther bros there?'

'Yeah, who do you wanna talk to?' 'Foof!' says Willo. 'Hang on …' comes the reply. 'Bouss, is dat you?'

'Yeah Willo,' replies Foof. Then he says, 'Bouss where are you? Get here quick! Something's going down. Grab a cab, Bouss! Or do you want me and King Kong to come and get ya?'

'Nah, I'll see ya there, Bouss,' says Willo, hanging up the phone. Willo goes back to the bar where his student mates are at the table. Willo announces he's leaving: 'Look guys, gotta go.' Picks up his bag and takes hold of his glass saying, 'One more for the road,' to his classmates, winks at them and downs his beer. 'Catcha later …' he says turning and heading for the door.

'Yeah, see ya later, mate.' 'Who's shot?' someone asks. Stepping out to a balmy Auckland evening, Willo is now in a totally different state of mind; like day and night; like student and gangster. Taking off his glasses and squinting, he even looks different. Willo never wears his glasses when he goes with his Black Panther bros. 'Bad for the image, you know, Bouss.' A lot of people mistake his bad eyesight for 'killer looks', even amongst his fellow Panther soldiers. He laughs to himself, 'Wonder wossup?' He muses further, 'Something to do with last week's first Battle of the Gangs, oops … First Battle of the Bands. Then again, it could be anything; been so much warring lately.'

Different gangs are trying to establish themselves and the Black Panthers are making sure they never take hold. Meanwhile, our fathers drink at the Gluepot, Ponsonby/Grey Lynn. 'This is our turf … Bring it on!'

Willo strides briskly on through K Road. It is busy now with the Thursday night shoppers, mostly brown and lots of kids. It is a habit with most Polynesian mums to take a couple of kids with them as a bit of a night out and also to help carry the shopping. Willo knows quite a few faces in the crowd. Here and there, along the way he meets up with and greets the ones he knows. Outside the Rising Sun he meets up with Regor and Heta. 'Owdy, Bouss. Got any koops,' says Heta shaking hands with Willo, who bursts out laughing: 'Not even a "How's your fucking day been?" I'm just a poor student, Bouss – been studying hard.' 'Yeah-yeah, studding more like it, with your arty-farty Palagi mates,' laughs Regor. And they all laugh. 'Bullshit man. That ain't true, Bouss.' 'Yeah yeah. Come on, we're all putting in for some booze. We gonna drink down at Western Park.'

Some of the TYs are there: Robin, Dave, Rat and

Image from *The Islanders* booklet. Auckland: Shortland Publications, NZ Newspapers Ltd, 1976, p.11.

a couple of others. Heta holds out his hand. Willo gives him $10, Regor, $20. Heta with a handful of cash then leads the way into the bottle store. While waiting for the attendant, Heta cracks a joke, 'Ayy Willo, what did DB say to Lion?' 'Don't know,' says Willo. 'Owdy, Bouss!' They all laugh. Only they knew what they were laughing at. 'Ha, ha, ha, ha, ha …'

Down past AGGs and cutting into a track leading directly into the heart of Western Park is their possie. To the right, further up on the opposite side, is the Taro Bar. Apart from the lampposts dotted about, there isn't much life about. And between the lampposts, it is quite dark. Especially on wintry nights with the fog … They hear the clinking of bottles. Willo gives out the Panther-whistle, which is returned almost like an echo. 'Up here, Bouss,' comes a voice from the darkness. It is Rat. 'Issat you Heta, Regor?' 'Yeah,' replies Regor. 'Who's with you?' asks Rat. 'Professor F.A.!' Heta laughs at Regor's joke. But Rat calls out, 'Good on you, Willo. Wondering where you been, Bouss.' 'Hooray Willo Bouss', chant the others. 'Long time no shee,' comes this other drunken slurring. 'Who dat?' asks Willo on arriving where they used to drink. Willo gets close before seeing it is Fleeps and Mickey. 'Ayy Bouss. Whaddaya mean, long time no see? I were at the Battle of the Gangs last week.' With that, all the Black Panthers have a good laugh. Bottles are opened. Conversation and booze flow on as they sit around the buttress roots of the huge old trees.

Willo starts talking about the plight of the Negroes in America, the race riots, etc. Most of [the] guys listen intently and understand. The general consensus is that all Rednecks should be shot. 'Better not come here and try that. Ayy, Bouss?' Willo goes on, 'It's already here, Bouss. You know the system. Look, I gotta a couple of books.

Here be Bobby Seale and …' 'Who the fuck's that?' snaps Regor. Willo answers, 'That's the guy that wrote the book called *Seize the Time*. See … here.' Willo holds up the book. They can't see it though; too dark. Regor goes on, 'Look Willo. It's all right for you at university – you can pull your books out there. But we're having a drink and getting ready to battle those cunts if they turn up …' 'Yeah well I'm here. That's why I'm here!' The vibe just changes. King Kong said, 'Wassamatter with you, Regor. I wouldn't mind reading Willo's book. Might learn sumpin …' 'Ayy sorry, Bouss,' says Regor, going over and hugging Willo. 'Ish OK, Bouss,' Willo

assures him. 'Drink up, Bouss.' 'Yay cheers.' They clink bottles: 'Panthers forever. Black Panthers!' All of them raise their fists in the murky shadowy light of Western Park. 'Let's have a drink to Sifi who will be getting out next week.' 'Yay! Here's to Sifi.' The booze flows. Henry, Rat and Foof go to get more.

About an hour later, they arrive back with an assortment of top shelf: whiskey, ouzo, vodka and a couple of girls; friends of Henry. The bros are praising the three that come back. But Heta is waving his finger at them and clucking his tongue like a Samoan dad, 'Boysh, yoush know ish akainst da larw.' Just then, one of the bros arrives. It is

Polynesian Panthers. From left to right: Fred Schmidt, Ta Iuli, Paul Dapp, Nooroa Teavae, Sam Vete. (Nigel Bhana photo archive).

Chero, breathlessly announcing: 'Those fellas are here. They're on a truck!' The Panthers rise up, some have bits of wood and all up and running to Ponsonby Road where Beaver and a couple of others front the Wehrmacht as they stand in front of the Taro Bar with softball bats.

The Wehrmacht are congregating beside the big work truck that is also their transport. All of them stand opposite the Taro Bar, eyeing up Beaver and the others, as they are starting to move across the road. Up from the park come the Panthers. 'Black Panthers!' some call out and then they are into it. Sandwiched on Ponsonby Road between the two Panther factions, the Wehrmacht are attacked front and back. Two or three bodies are already out cold on the road. Like the week before, they panic and scatter, running away and up Ponsonby Road towards K Road, leaving behind the big Bedford truck which belongs to them. Down Newton Gully run the chasers. The guys running away are starting to undress as they run: discarding jackets, jerseys and even Beatle boots; no good for running in (heh-heh). The Blue is over in less than a minute after the first couple went down. It is 'Good-bye Pork Pie …' For that to happen, it has to be fast, vicious and focused. The Panthers for the most part are all half cut from the booze, but at the moment of the strike, they were in complete control; moving as one.

Meanwhile, around the back of the Taro Bar, beside the wee bakery, Panthers are knocking back the piss. A couple more are coming up from the Suffolk. On being told that they missed out on the Blue, they are clearly hacked off. One of the other guys says, 'What are we gonna do with this fucking truck?' 'We'll go for a ride!' says another. A chorus of laughter from all around. The truck is eventually taken and hidden in one of the family houses down in Herne Bay.

All is good and they have some chicks as well … It is decided to shift the drinking to Toa's house down Williamson Ave where some of the Brothers have already gone, coz of the cops arriving. Toa's is where the party is in full swing: Hendrix blasting out of the stereo. Toa's place, a two-bedroom flat, is already chocker and even more so with the arrival of the rest of the Panthers, so there is hardly any room. Toa opens up the French doors that lead to the balcony. Willo, King Kong and others propped up there, opening a box of beer and passing it around the crew.

One of the Senior Panthers, Sefo, turns the stereo off. 'Let's sing some songs. It ain't a party with no singing. Bring the gat. Give it to Foof. What's a song I wanna sing.' Sefo starts singing, 'She wears my ring, to show the …' 'Wrong key,' says Foof. Sefo is in the middle of the lounge trying to match his voice to the given chord. All the younger Panthers are smiling amongst themselves at the choice of song by Sefo. Especially as his wife has left him for another bloke while he was in the nick. The younger members know the story: Sefo still carries a torch for his ex.

'Play another song' someone suggests. 'Never mind all that broken-arse, pese shit.' Sefo looks visibly hurt at this comment but doesn't let on. Instead he grabs the whiskey and starts drinking it straight. 'Come on, Bouss, play "Stone Free".' Foof plays the request but Sefo is not happy with the new music that his younger bros are into. Still, everyone is singing. Plenty of piss, that's all that matters. However, Sefo misses the bros his own age. At least they know the songs he likes. All this new music he terms, 'hippy music', belonging, he thinks, to those drug-taking, flea-ridden hippies, who appeared outta nowhere it seems … How the world is changing. He thinks of Samoa. No, he didn't wanna go down that road. 'Big party next week for Sifi. OK, boys?' 'Yeah!' Those that hear him agree. 'When's he out?' pops the question from someone. 'Next year,' replies Sefo. 'Now, how about my song Foof?' 'I've got one,' he replies. 'All right which one then?' asks Sefo.

Sefo starts to sing, 'She wears my ring …' All the younger Panthers look at each other, smiling, knowingly and singing along with their older Panther Brother. Sefo is a good fighter; a soldier from way back. Just like Sifi. But the respect for Sefo, just like the respect for Sifi, is not out of fear, but for the Polynesian culture of respect to their elders. This respect is the workings of their New Zealand street family: the Black Panthers.

Outside the French doors leading to the balcony is Willo talking about the Black Panther movement in the States. King Kong is perusing *Seize the Time*. One of the boys stands by the doors, listening to Willo while Regor joins in and goes on about what the Negroes are going through. The argument is whether the United States situation can be compared to the Polynesians in Grey Lynn/Ponsonby and, more generally, in New Zealand.

'Look,' says Regor, 'We don't have to sit in the back of buses. We're allowed to vote. Plenty of work if you want it. No problem …' 'Yeah, that's all very well!' blurts out Willo. 'But there are parallels to our people here in Aotearoa. It's just not so blatant. Look at what they have done to our Maori brothers.' 'That's their own fault!' counters Regor. 'Too busy fighting amongst themselves.' 'Nah, I don't buy that. It's the system; it's an all white thing. You know, "Divide and Rule". We just don't see it. Look at all our brothers in jail …'

'I'd really like to get something happening for our people in the area. I'd also like to get something happening for our bros in jail.' Willo stops and takes a swig of his beer with King Kong and Captain Fred nodding in agreement. This makes Regor angry and he goes on the offensive: 'You think cos you're at varsity, you know everything ayy Willo!' Willo looks up at Regor, squinting as he always does without his glasses and getting up, off his chair, saying he has to pee …

As he is about to go inside, Pita blind shots Willo on the side of his head beside his ear. Willo falls over the lounge, onto the table that holds the top shelf, glasses and bottles. It breaks his fall. Willo springs up and goes for Pita, punching and grappling. Both of them smash through the railing of the balcony and fall several feet onto the front lawn. Everyone comes out to break it up but Sefo belts Pita. And then King Kong smacks Sefo. Toa ends up hitting his missus who is on at him about him and his mates and what is going down; screaming her head off, and threatening to ring the cops. Foof and some of the others, who aren't fighting, manage to stop the Blue, though the bros are still yelling at each other.

Sefo speaks first: 'Look at me! Look at what you done to me! You, no respect. I'm your elder. Sifi's not gonna like this. We're the ones you follow!' He starts to cry. So does Regor. Not Willo: 'Nahh, Bouss. You know how it always ends up. I'm sick of it Bouss! You know I wanna do something different, something for our people, our Brothers in jail. If our people done up themselves and their houses it would be worth heaps. Imagine it, Bouss.' Someone else pipes up, 'Just like it was the Bronx where we'd get shafted. It will always be the Bronx!' Willo continues, 'You gotta have a vision, Bouss. Any ways you can.'

'Yeah,' Regor talking, 'I'm sick of your killer looks!' 'Bouss, don't you know I need glasses?

Only I don't wear them around the bros. I leave them for uni', replies Willo. 'You know – bad for the image.' With that Regor laughs and becomes quite emotional. He goes over and hugs Willo. Everybody is making up and the vibe mellows somewhat. Foof plays 'Proud Mary' – 'Looking for a job in the city …' The party goes on. Willo sits next to King Kong and Captain.

Regor comes over, slurring a bit. He says to Willo, 'You know, you're right bout watcha said but what can I do about it? The cops know me. I never got past form two. Not like you, Bouss. You're at uni. Good on ya, if you wanna do something. Besides, Willo, you do it for us, all the bros here ayy?' King Kong and Captain nod in agreement.

'We still wanna be known as Panthers though. And you can't take the Black Panthers.' 'No, I know,' nods Willo. 'Maybe Polynesian Panthers. Who knows?' he adds. Regor nods, 'That's sweet ayy?' Regor turns to Heta, 'Bouss, Willo wants to start the Polynesian Panthers and help clean up Ponsonby/ Grey Lynn. Take all our rubbish to da dump, get rid of all the rats.' They laugh … 'Serious Bouss.' Willo calls out, 'What do ya think?' Foof stops playing with all eyes on Willo who is now standing next to Regor (both bearing wounds from each other's fists). Foof suggests free transport for families to visit jails. More laughter. 'No, he's right.' Willo goes on, 'We can get these things; just gotta fight for it … Wouldn't it be great if say Sifi's family wants to visit him? The camps are so far away for him, his missus and kid. And you know, we gotta treat our women with a bit more *alofa*. Connie, one of the girls, says, 'Yeah Willo, so true.' Meanwhile someone asks, 'Where's Toa and his missus?' 'They went for a walk.' Someone says, 'Fuck, did ya hear her?' 'That's what I mean, Bouss,' Willo starts up again.

Sefo asks Foof to play 'Ring of Fire'. 'Who da hell sings that?' Foof winks at Heta and plays the chorus straight away. 'From the start. From the start,' pleads Sefo. Connie is nodding off and is leaning against Henry. Henry whispers something in her ear and then they both disappear into Toa's bedroom.

Soon after, the bedsprings are creaking. All is quiet. 'Shhhh.' A few minutes later Henry is out, 'Your turn, Bouss.' He indicates to Willo. 'Nah,' Willo declines, shaking his head. But someone else jumps in. It is Heta. From the bedroom, Connie yells out, 'Henry you promised!' and starts crying. Heta hits her and she starts screaming. Now Heta is really giving it to her and some of the bros go in. 'Come on, Heta – no need for that!' they're saying. Willo looks at King Kong and clucks his tongue. 'Yeah, Bouss. See what I mean. This ain't me, Bouss,' Willo says, standing up. 'I'm off.' 'We're coming too, Bouss. We're with you …'

Willo, King Kong, Captain Fred, Pauly and Aro walk out with the big drama going on in the bedroom. Up the street, they bump into Toa and his missus. 'Yous off, Bouss?' he inquires. 'Yeah,' replies King Kong. 'What's happening?' 'Your bedroom is getting wrecked. Henry put Connie on the Block. She wouldn't wear it with Heta so he's bashed her up.' 'Bugger off … Cops will be along soon. You better get to your house or what's left of it …'

At Surrey Cres they part company, agreeing to get together at Captain Fred's place. Not really about what and why; maybe somewhere, where they can really drink in peace without fighting each other. Within themselves they know they've come to a crossroads of sorts. As to the lifestyle in their Black Panther Brotherhood, each one would die for the other and yet, paradoxically, turn on each other at the slightest excuse.

They think of what Toa was talking about earlier on. 'But that's the way warriors test each other. If you are a proud warrior you stand up to it. I guess too many warriors in one place and full of booze. What do you expect?' However, the camaraderie remains to this day. 'Fa sole, Willo.' 'Fa, Bouss', says King Kong to his Brother Panthers. 'Hey, Kong! What did Lion say to DB? Ha ha ha!' Willo and King Kong laugh out loud while going their separate ways; King Kong to King Street and Willo out to Sandringham. He ain't been home since he left for uni the day before.

Willo makes those clucking noises to himself and shakes his head as if to say no. He thinks of Sifi in the nick and tries to guestimate Sifi's opinion of him. Willo has great respect for Sifi who was one of the first Island kids to arrive in New Zealand. He was part of the first wave of migrant families to step off the boat onto the streets of Ponsonby in the late forties, early fifties. In the eyes of his own community and in the System they are living in, Sifi and others in the same situation would be termed as non-achievers; especially now with a police record; Willo being the exception in their lot.

Willo is certain that Sifi wouldn't object to his vision of getting things happening on a socio-political level for 'Our' people. Suggesting things like hanging onto their properties in the inner city of Auckland. 'No,' thinks Willo. 'Sifi would be proud of him. After all, he and all the other bros ensured that he, Willo, would be free of any kind of form with the Cops, and now Uni. It's still hip to 'know'. But not all knowledge could be got from books. Books don't teach experience; a 'been there thing'. Willo concludes, 'I'll need to explain it in more detail when Sifi gets out.'

And it isn't just a question of explaining it to himself. Here's King Kong, Captain Fred, Aro and Pauly. They can all see what Willo is on about. Willo feels positive: 'Gotta go up, man! Power to the people! Don't wanna be lost in fretful thoughts at all.'

Willo always had a problem with the way the Palagi media differentiates between the brown peoples in New Zealand, as a whole, in most news stories on crime. Quote: 'The offender is either Maori or Pacific Islander.' 'The media figures that Aotearoa is two large islands in the South Pacific, inhabited by Polynesian people from Hawaii to Easter Island. But to all Polynesians, this is brown Man's part of the world. The ocean is our prairie. Your horse is our cart. The media should just call all of us Polynesians, just like their Caucasians is all inclusive; someone from Sweden through to another from either Spain or Greece. Funny that. Same old hidden agenda: "Divide and Rule." We gotta get everyone together, especially all the Polynesians. That's it!' Willo has a brainwave.

'Haka, Hula, Tamure, Meke, Lakalaka right through to Siva. All covered under "Polynesian Panthers". That'll get everyone; all of our young people together. Then we can get started to address the needs of our people. If this is what being educated is all about, then Sifi and his so-called negative bros, helped him in their own way to put him there. So he and the four other bros who left with him are gonna go hard; only more with a pen than a bat. For now at least anyways. The attitude is definitely from the street. Especially if learnt from someone who left an impact in one's make-up, with direction and leadership. What to do in certain street situations; growing up in a foreign country where nepotism and racist attitudes fly at you in all guises. You know: looks, eyes, double-meaning sentences, body language. All that shit; all that redneck shit.

'Sifi had the attitude that we as young fellas understood. He was "hands-on" as well. They say the quality of leadership is to serve. Sifi had served us by not just having the right attitude, but by throwing the first punch, whenever a bad vibe was coming towards us. Never mind whether we were outnumbered or not; it was just ku'i. Sifi had the big heart and we respected that. If anyone needed taking out for whatever reason, Sifi only had to give the nod. After a while, it was always a race to see who got the first punch in and always going for the "Killer Hook" almost straight away. Trouble is, all or most of the bros have been tainted in the eyes of the System. To change the status quo, ya gotta be in there. This is the angle it's gonna go by.'

Willo is certain Sifi wouldn't want the next generation of young Polynesians heading where he, Sifi, is. Also knowing Sifi's heart and far-sightedness, he'd be rapt knowing one of his protégés from the street is gonna do it legally. And for our people, coz it is way too late for Sifi himself to go that way. Still, if Willo is there, they will all be there. Everyone wants to be on the winning side, but they can't all be winners. Someone has to run with the losers. When our people left the islands, some often left something behind besides the tropical weather. In fact many actually lost something on departure. This'll be what Sifi would have said. Sifi's not only good with his fists but is also a great thinker.

Willo is confident within himself: 'Polynesian Panthers. Hmmm … It's gotta nice ring to it. The time is right.' Willo thinks of his Bouss, Foof, and one of the tunes he was playing. 'Bring out the instigator, because there's something in the air – We gotta get together sooner or later, cos the Revolution's here …' It is appropriate for the mood Willo is in. 'And you know it's right!!!' Willo chuckles to himself on New North Road. He stops and waits for the Sandringham bus to take him home. And on the bus, Willo pulls out pen and paper and starts the arduous task of working out a strategy. First of all, making a list of things to do: meetings, public speaking, recruitment drive, youth to adult members and women members. Willo knows two or three women who are in such a frame of mind. Liaison is a must … He thinks, 'Getting these women on board would be a great asset.' In noting that down, he will contact them as soon as possible. Feeling tired now from the lack of sleep, Willo closes his eyes and relaxes, visualising all that he has been thinking about.

Definitely a man on a mission, Willo thinks about calling a meet with the four Bouss and put this paper to them: to collectively brainstorm the aims and objectives of the Polynesian Panthers. It has to be quite clear to everyone: the 'why and the wherefore'; the philosophy of the group. Women must feel safe in the organisation. But will everyone be happy with the name – Polynesian Panthers? He'll know that when he meets up with King Kong and the others.

The following Tuesday, 16 June 1971, is the first meeting at Captain Fred's place. Three new faces are identified to the call. Captain Fred is to become the first president. All agreed. The name Polynesian Panthers; the need for a base – these are some of the issues raised. Also, no booze at meetings.

In no time, an office is established above some shops at the end of Ponsonby Road in Three Lamps. Also joining are three dynamic Polynesian sisters who passionately believe in the kaupapa. They have roles in public speaking and running a youth recruitment drive.

There is one incident at the Mt Albert Shopping Centre. Sister Ma'a of the Polynesian Panthers is giving the spiel about the social issues concerning her Polynesian people. But this only brings out anger and resistance from the shop owners. Still, a crowd gathers around this beautiful Polynesian goddess with her big afro and boar's tooth necklace. She speaks the Queen's English perfectly and has an instant rapport with the mostly brown-faced audience.

Here and there are Palagi of the hippy/student variety, holding sticks of incense. Another one in the crowd is a local lad, Kavika, who is living on the edge. He could go either way any time. He is that kind of person that gets bored real ezy and always on the go. But it is a fact that Kavika is taken aback by Sister Ma'a; he is not used to seeing a woman, especially a brown woman, speaking in public. His idea of women is that they are subservient to the men as the case with his own ma and pa. It is that way in Samoa …

As he listens, he thinks, 'This lady has some valid points, especially on issues like the value of property around Grey Lynn and Ponsonby.' Kavika wants more info so he waits till this lady finishes her speech on the Polynesian Panther Youth Movement. But as she gets off the podium, she is confronted by a couple of media people who are keen to get a story. Kavika has to wait some more. When they finally leave, Kavika makes his way towards her. Ma'a sees this strong, good-looking, young man approaching. 'I liked what you had to say,' utters Kavika, breaking the ice. 'I think you are really brave; you're the first "Islander Woman" that I have ever seen, get up like you did.'

'I'm mouldy,' she retorts. 'We're all the same I reckon,' says Kavika, thinking he has put his foot in his mouth. But she understands. 'Kia ora to that!' continues Ma'a with this young man. Kavika, realising how beautiful Ma'a is close up, is suddenly, totally lost for words. She rescues him by asking if he wants to join up with them (the Polynesian Panther Youth Movement). 'Come on,' she insists, 'Come, and do something positive for your people.'

Coming from her, how can he refuse? Kavika soon joins up with the Polynesian Panther Youth.

'After here, I'll take you to see my senior Polynesian Panther Brothers. You'll meet up with King Kong, Willo, Pauly, Aro and our President, Captain Fred. And others you might have heard of when they were in the Black Panthers. Now they have started up the Polynesian Panthers – to do something positive. To make changes for the better. Even physically fight for our rights. Justice! Wherever we are needed …'

'Yeah!! That's for me,' says Kavika with a smile.

ENDNOTES

1 Walker, R. (11 December, 1982) in *Korero*. Cited in Satele, M. F. (1998) *The Polynesian Panthers: An Assertion of Ethnic and Cultural Identities through Activism in Auckland during the 1970s.* Unpublished MA thesis, Education, University of Auckland, p.73.

2 Excerpt, with minor editing, from Anae, M. (2004) 'From Kava to Coffee: The "Browning" of Auckland'. In Carter, I., Craig, D. and Matthewman, S. (Eds) *Almighty Auckland?* Palmerston North: Dunmore Press.

3 Excerpt from Luafutu, Fa'amoana John (1994) A Boy Called Broke: My Story, So Far. Christchurch: Macmillan Brown Centre for Pacific Studies, University of Canterbury.

PART FOUR

FROM GANG TO POLYNESIAN PANTHER MOVEMENT

As Part Three has indicated, among New Zealand-born Pacific peoples a typical response to racist taunts at school and in the wider community was to join a gang or another marginal group. Here they could vent their anger, disillusionment and sense of inadequacy, fuelled by a feeling that they had no control over their lives. Another outlet for these feelings – and a means of addressing the cause of them – was the Polynesian Panther Movement (PPM).

The Polynesian Panther Movement was founded in 1971 by a group of Pacific Islanders – Samoans, Tongans, Cook Islanders – and a few Māori. Many were university students when they became Panthers. Most had grown up and still lived in inner-city Auckland. Their families were typically of lower socio-economic status, and some families belonged to Newton Church in Ponsonby.

For many Panther members, political awareness had begun early. Pacific youth could not help but become enmeshed in the political stand-off between the dominant group of mainstream New Zealanders and the smaller group of tangata whenua who were demanding their sovereign rights under the Treaty of Waitangi. Many began to support Māori political initiatives (such as the Bastion Point occupation and Waitangi Day protests) while still at secondary school. Often those who joined Māori groups became skilled in political lobbying and political processes, and used these skills to assert their own Pacific identity and raise the profile of Pacific peoples in New Zealand. Not surprisingly, initial involvement and association with Māori liberation groups and activists provided the impetus for some to later take initiatives for change for Pacific peoples.

Because of their working-class background, most New Zealand-borns from an early age were also aware that government policies concerning Pacific peoples were ineffectual and they understood issues relating to unequal pay and unsatisfactory working conditions. It was often through their parents' involvement that Panthers first became familiar with the Labour Party, protest, trade unions and marches.

Against this background, the PPM – propelled by stimulating and inspirational leaders – provided an opportunity for New Zealand-borns to express their solidarity with the Māori liberation struggle, and to express their own identity as Pacific peoples. For some members, the movement was a vehicle for 'conscientising' their people. For some, it was a vehicle for fundamental, radical change – specifically, the overthrow of the capitalist system, which they saw as responsible for the oppression of Pacific peoples in New Zealand.[1] In members' words, the PPM was a 'social conscience' and a stand saying, 'We're not going to take it any more'.[2]

As it declared through its stated goals, PPM was concerned with the welfare of Pacific peoples at every level. Once its headquarters in Ponsonby were established, the movement's work began in earnest. Panthers ran homework centres and made school visits; they visited Pacific prisoners in Paremoremo and hired buses to take along the prisoners' families if they had no transport of their own; they ran programmes informing Pacific peoples of their legal rights as New Zealand citizens. They even organised community social events: PPM street parties, supported by the Auckland City Council, brought together at-risk gang members and unemployed youth in Ponsonby and Grey Lynn. Before long, the PPM was expanding both nationally and further afield, with chapters in South Auckland, Christchurch, Dunedin, and Sydney, Australia.

The PPM also supported Māori political initiatives and movements: some of its members were also foundation members of Ngā Tamatoa. In 1972, the PPM joined with Ngā Tamatoa, the Stormtroopers, Head Hunters and Tihei Mauriora to form 'a loose Polynesian Front'. In 1974, this united 'Polynesian Front' was consolidated with support from more Māori and Polynesian progressive organisations. The Panthers became

A talk given by Wayne Toleafou-Peseta Minister of Information of the Polynesian Panther Movement.

Craccum, 14 September 1972.

involved in opposition to the 1981 Springbok Tour (collaborating with groups such as Halt All Racist Tours [HART]), as well as joining the Māori Land March in 1975, Treaty of Waitangi protest marches and marches to promote the recognition of te reo Māori as one of New Zealand's two official languages. In publicising the everyday struggles of Māori and Pacific peoples – struggles that ranged from land claims to police discrimination and violence – PPM sought a pan-ethnic grouping of Māori and Pacific peoples. Yet here the group's views conflicted with those of Ngā Tamatoa, who prioritised Māori unity.

The reflections and recollections that follow show how the PPM grew from the ground up in response to the victimisation of Pacific peoples in inner-city Auckland. The Panthers were quick to form collaborations and synergies with other community groups for the purposes of lobbying for community resources and exposing racist attitudes and practices of both the Palagi system and individuals. As these accounts also make clear, the Panthers successfully galvanised a true multicultural community spirit in Ponsonby. Local rag the *West End News*, for example, was translated into Samoan, Cook Islands Māori and Niuean as a way of meeting the needs of its growing Pacific communities. Moreover, the Panthers actively published articles in the *West End News* to clear up some of the misconceptions some of the community held concerning the PPM, and also at times received positive publicity in articles published in the *New Zealand Herald* detailing its emergence and ideologies.

During these crucible years, the Polynesian Panthers flourished in being seen and heard around Auckland. Their lobbying against racism and for changes produced real results. The setting up of a chapter in Sydney by Will and a few other Panthers caused world headlines when Will was arrested.

Panther Twenty-nine

WAYNE TOLEAFOA

My membership number was 29, indicating that 28 other people had joined what was then known as the Black Panther Movement (New Zealand) before me. I was not one of the founders but was attracted by what the movement stood for. In my 17-year-old mind, the Black Panthers in the United States stood for many things, including militantly opposing racism (in its personal and institutional forms), addressing injustices against oppressed groups and particularly opposing right-wing racist groups such as the Ku Klux Klan.

New Zealand in the 1970s was certainly not the United States, but it was also not the harmonious society that many older Pākehā

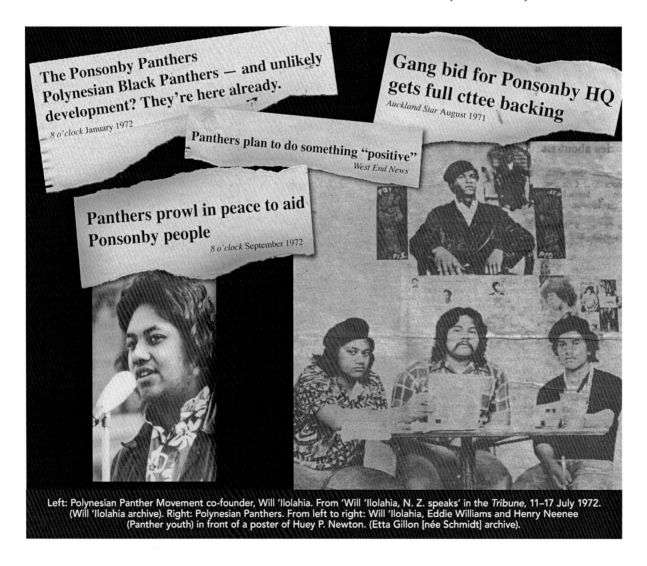

The Ponsonby Panthers
Polynesian Black Panthers — and unlikely development? They're here already.
8 o'clock January 1972

Gang bid for Ponsonby HQ gets full cttee backing
Auckland Star August 1971

Panthers plan to do something "positive"
West End News

Panthers prowl in peace to aid Ponsonby people
8 o'clock September 1972

Left: Polynesian Panther Movement co-founder, Will 'Ilolahia. From 'Will 'Ilolahia, N. Z. speaks' in the *Tribune*, 11–17 July 1972. (Will 'Ilolahia archive). Right: Polynesian Panthers. From left to right: Will 'Ilolahia, Eddie Williams and Henry Neenee (Panther youth) in front of a poster of Huey P. Newton. (Etta Gillon [née Schmidt] archive).

wanted to believe it was. If you were Māori, or a Pacific Islander, you soon learned that you were not regarded as an equal by many Pākehā And often that judgement was based on race, rather than a lack of ability, or on flaws in your character.

It was not until I attended secondary school that I began to notice the racist jibes – 'black bastards', 'nig nogs' and so on – that all Islanders and Māori are familiar with. The disappointing thing about these racist jibes was that they came from the minds and mouths of Pākehā boys who had adopted these racist views from their parents' generation. As well as being demeaning, their jibes indicated the poor quality of the relationship between many Pākehā and Polynesians and the gap between fact and myth.

The quality of this relationship is clearly illustrated by the National Party's election campaign advertising, in which an angry, threatening Pacific Island male (with floral shirt and Afro hairstyle) grasped a broken beer bottle in his hand –an inaccurate but popular image of the Pacific Islanders (and Māori) among many Pākehā. The infamous Dawn Raids too created a climate of mistrust between Pacific communities and wider Pākehā society. They left me and many other Pacific Islanders with a sense of vulnerability and aloneness.

Economically, numerically and in almost every statistic, Pacific Islanders were also shown as the most vulnerable group in New Zealand society. This is not where we wanted to be.

To many young Polynesians like myself, the only way forward for us as a migrant people was 'self-help'. We would have to stand up for ourselves and for our people, and not wait for others to do it for us. In my mind, at that time,

the Black Panthers (New Zealand) provided the platform for us to do just that.

What made it easy to join the Panthers was that it was Ponsonby-based. Ponsonby of the 1960s and 1970s was something like Mangere or Otara of the present. There was a definite migrant flavour about it. The fruit shops and grocers sold Polynesian foods. Wearing a *lava lava*, or an aloha shirt was not seen as donning a national costume; it was the everyday wear of the Pacific Islands, where our parents came from. There was the feeling of being 'at home' in Ponsonby, although I remember laughing when I overheard two Pākehā bus drivers refer to the Ponsonby bus route as 'the Congo run'. That comment was indicative of what many Pākehā thought of Ponsonby back then. I was a 'native' of Ponsonby and proud of it.

The small Panther office in Ponsonby Road soon became the hangout for a lot of teenage members like myself. Will 'Ilolahia was our chairman, who I thought of as an 'older person' (at the ripe old age of 19). I eventually became the minister of information of the renamed Polynesian Panther Movement. I left the movement after only two years, to concentrate on my studies which had fallen way behind, partly because of my involvement in the PPM. (I eventually graduated with a BA in history.)

During my two years of active involvement with the PPM, I had some great and challenging experiences which left me feeling old at 19. I helped organise and took part in protest marches involving thousands of people. I was almost arrested several times although I [was] always careful to act within the law. I and other Panther members spoke at several public protest rallies and numerous smaller meetings alongside older (and politically more aware) people like

Tom Newnham, Trevor Richards, Joris de Bres, Tim Shadbolt and Oliver Sutherland. We also counted among our allies, 'radicals' such as Tame Iti, Roger Fowler, Syd Jackson (and Ngā Tamatoa) and even former Prime Minister Helen Clark, who was involved in university student politics of the time. A brilliant Auckland lawyer called David Lange, prime minister 1984–89) even helped us put together a 'Your Rights' legal aid booklet. The PPM was only one small political group among many in an era of protest throughout the Western world. The difference between us and

homework centres in Auckland to help younger Polynesians to succeed at school by linking them up with other academically 'successful' young Polynesians. About 20 young students would come to these classes every week.

Some saw us as simply another gang because we wore black as a kind of uniform and we tended to travel in groups. Some of our older members like Eddie Williams, Fred Schmidt, Vaughn Sanft, Nooroa Teavae, Will 'Ilolahia, Henry Nee Nee and many of our supporters, were in fact former gang members and were sometimes recognised

City & West End News   March 1973

Legal rights booklet selling fast. More than 600 copies of a booklet on citizens' legal rights were sold last week

other radical groups in New Zealand was that we saw ourselves as a Pan-Pacific movement, which welcomed Māori and peoples from all Pacific Islands. Some Pākehā were members or official supporters. We also had Indian and Chinese members or supporters. We were certainly not a black (or brown) supremacist group as many people supposed.

We were also generally a well-educated group of young people. Like our parents, many of us saw education as one of the keys to advancement for Polynesian people. We started one of the first

by members of hostile rival gangs. And even though some of us younger members had never been gang members, we found ourselves fighting for the Panther pride, or looking for the nearest fire escape to avoid getting a hiding from some of the hostile gangs. I was a firm believer in 'living to fight another day' and was never in favour of violent solutions. But to many of our contemporaries, we were a political gang and a target.

We did, however, enjoy the support of the Ponsonby gangs of the time, and the Storm

Troopers of Otara. It was great to count them among our friends, as they too sought to improve the lot of Māori and Pacific Island youths in South Auckland. Like the Storm Troopers, we were often walking that fine line between being a do-gooder social service and a serious political protest group. The PPM also provided much of my social life, outside of Church and family, and marked a formative 'growing up' period for many of us younger members.

I will always remember my time in the Panthers as a time of openness, when I encountered for the first time some of the diversity that is New Zealand society. I went to my first gay party while I was in the Panthers. Met and mixed with women from the women's liberation movement. Heard, for the first time, the voice of Māori youth, even though I had lived in New Zealand all my life. It was also stimulating to meet with people of other political persuasions, from Trotskyists to Muldoonists, at parties and other social gatherings. My Panther friends and I discussed and grappled with youthful issues like values, drugs, sexuality, spirituality, relationships, identity, freedom and music. Some of us became very close because of this experience and I still feel that closeness today, whenever I meet them.

Time has a modifying influence. Today I still believe that we did the right thing, by raising issues such as racism and the importance of preserving Māori and Pacific cultures. I still believe that the way forward for Māori and Pacific Islanders comes through self-help. What I am happy with is that many Pākehā now see with the same eyes. I also see now that being a New Zealander means appreciating the European heritage that is a huge part of the New Zealand identity, and that we now share a common destiny.

The recollections of an investigator
'THE SHILLOUETTE'

The local community paper came out with a photo of a group of people who I recognised as role models and some that I knew were members of a local gang call the Nigs. Among them was Ta Iuli, the sort of PI that looked and talked like a PI. One day when I met him, he said he was preparing himself for School Cert so I asked him about sitting the upcoming exam and how the swotting was going. To my astonishment, Ta revealed that he did not need to swot and that the exam would be a walk in the park. I had never been exposed to that kind of confidence before, from a Samoan. I found it unnerving, almost to the point of disbelief. To be that confident was almost showing off, but coming from Ta that seemed normal. Needless to say, Ta fulfilled his prophecy. So I was somewhat not surprised to see Ta as the minister of information, in this beret-wearing group that called itself the Polynesian Panthers: a gang that wasn't a Gang.

Another who was notable in the group was Will 'Ilolahia. I had known him as a prefect at Mt Albert Grammar School but not personally. I was suspicious and wary of him because he represented the authorities at the school. Seeing this unified group photo together with their various titles seemed to give them some mana … and I held them in awe.

Much later someone mentioned one night that the Polynesian Panthers were looking to form a military wing. I was knocking around with a loose group of street kids of mixed PIs and Māori who called themselves the Junior Nigs. I never considered myself a member, just an associate.

One evening, a group of us appeared outside the Panthers' HQ on the corner of College Hill and Ponsonby Road. The main glass front entrance of the buildings led into the former ANZ Bank. To the right of the building on the Ponsonby Road side were tall, double-panelled kauri doors which seemed to me to lead forever up those long, creaky steps to the HQ. At the top of the stairs a yellow light glowed, beckoning … Moving shadows betrayed activity that crossed from room to room across the upstairs

Through the doorway, past the local rag that shared the upstairs area with the PPP, I was impressed with the quality of the sisters and the brothers who were registered PPP members. The industrious paper shuffling of the sisters breathed organisation into the area upstairs. It felt like a busy organisation. These were people I recognised from primary, league, Grammar, the hood and Church. They had a sense of direction, a certainty of where they were going, achievers among our peers.

Christchurch Star　　　　　　　　　　　　　June 1973

Homework Centre Proposal To Aid Young Polynesians

hallway. To enter that light brought apprehension and loss of confidence. It overwhelmed me; a whirlpool of emotions flashed through me; commitment to something other than the family – inconceivable!

And besides that, I now had my comfort zone: I felt strong; I had no big plans; I had no future! The eternal 'now' was all that counted. I could handle myself. My confidence was my ability to handle myself physically. I did not seek trouble but I could protect myself! And to minimise any collateral damage my instincts told me to hear my own counsel: more bad decision making than good. Any obligation to the PPP would have to be spectacular: the heart pounded and the mind sped like a street blue; eyes wide open, poised to react.

The black crew neck jerseys and the berets projected solidarity and uniformity. The young members of our multicultural community were being brought together by other younger members. I liked what I saw but felt out of place, weird. I was impatient, agitated. Where is the recruitment? Let's get it on! Where is my mission?

A lasting impression was a large portrait on the wall, showing a defiant Angela Davies with the caption: 'The only difference between society and a criminal is the criminal got caught.' I liked that rhythm but action was what I needed: something to rage against the system. I may have dropped by the HQ once again but we had all moved on consciously – one thought or another.

Some sort of street party was organised by the PPP outside the Leys Institute Library one evening. I had been hanging out with family members of The Face, a Māori Band from up north (Mark Williams on vocals, Willie Hona guitar) who played the gig at the street party. I was standing around trying to get into the picture. Another PPP occasion was at the Ponsonby Community Centre. A lot of big dudes wearing leather jackets and berets amassed out front. For some reason there was a lot of tension and aggravation in the air that night. Being 15 or

16 at the time, you had to be careful not to stare directly at anyone. Then, hostilities boiled over into minor skirmishes. The swearing and disorderly behaviour continued up Ponsonby Terrace and onto Ponsonby Road where one of the Warau brothers set about smashing shop windows along the Ponsonby Strip. This only served to fuel my cynical attitude towards the social aspirations of the PPP.

Thursdays on K Road was always amazing; the sea of brown PI people moving, bumping, laughing and shopping on that strip. There was something energising and spiritual about K Road then. Tigi Ness and Ama Rauhihi had hitched up during that period and I could not work out the attraction and the genuine affection Tigi showed towards Ama. Then, on Thursday night outside the main entrance of the St Kevin's Arcade, a group of PPP members and associates congregated for a rally. Ama got on the soapbox with the bull horn speaker and spoke. Instantly, like a revelation, I understood the reason for Tigi's passion for Ama. There were loftier, nobler aspirations in the meeting of the minds. I believe that this was the first time I can genuinely say that I respected a woman.

Do they WANT us to roam the streets?

The sit-in demonstration on Friday night was disappointing not because of the lack of concern by the participants, but by the public

City & West End News March 1972

'Do they want us to roam the streets?' Panthers protesting about the need for more public facilities for Polynesian youth in the city. Tigilau Ness holding placard. Auckland: *City and West End News*, 22 March, 1972, p.3.

Interview with Tigilau Ness

TIGILAU NESS TALKS WITH LITO VILISONI, NATIONAL RADIO

At 17 years of age, Tigi joined the Polynesian Panthers. In the following interview he talks to Lito Vilisoni, who is also from Niue.

Tigi: I was expelled from Mount Albert Grammar for not cutting my hair. I had an Afro (quite big), because at the time Jimi Hendrix was the icon for a lot of black people and it was a source of pride and something to stand up for and say: 'Hey, this is me', as compared to Brylcreem on fuzzy hair. (Tigi and Lito laugh.) You know, 'Keep the hair straight – Go to school and all that; Brylcreem, Brylcreem, Brylcreem.' Yeah, well at Mount Albert Grammar I was pulled up by the headmaster one day. He told me, 'Ness, you'd better get a hair cut.' And I said, 'But this is my culture; we grow the eldest boy's hair long and then we have a hair cutting ceremony.' He told me, 'No, you get it cut or you're out!' And I said, 'Well stuff your school, I'm out!'

Well, as I was walking out the front gate of Mount Albert Grammar, there was a whole lot of Auckland University students protesting: 'Racist school! Racist school!' People like Tim Shadbolt, Will 'Ilolahia were there all because I wouldn't cut my hair.

Lito: Where did you go from there?

Tigi: For one or two years I kicked around in the streets. I was virtually unemployable; just leaving school with no skills … One night, out late, we were just sitting around … and this young Samoan boy, Mapu Iuli, says to me, 'Ayy, bro, you should come and join the Polynesian Panthers. They are really doing good things, helping people.' And I thought, 'Oh yeah, sounds good.' It's not a gang because at that time gangs were the thing that a lot of Pacific Island and Māori children or youth got into; there was nothing else to do.

Today it's completely different; you have got a whole lot of languages and cultural awareness. Back then we were more or less forced into trying to be something that we weren't. And the saying in the Panthers back then was, 'You got one foot in the taro patch and one foot in the garage …'

Lito: So were you able to fulfil some of that emotional, spiritual hunger when you joined the Panthers and started kicking around with people like Will. Who else was around?

Tigi: Melani Anae, Etta Schmidt and Lyn Doherty. Lyn was one of the Māori women in the Polynesian Panthers, which was predominantly Pacific Island but we felt we were all Polynesian. Just that the Māori came here by canoe and we came later on by jet. There was also Miriama Rauhihi (whom I ended up marrying and having three children to, Ché Fu, hip hop artist being the eldest)

Lito: What sort of disciplines were you learning then from the Panthers?

Tigi: Well, I first talked to Mapu Iuli about the Panthers … He figured I was brainy because I read books and all that kind of stuff. He said, 'Read this book by Eldridge Cleaver, Soul on Ice (he was a Black Panther). So I read it and wanted more. Up till then I had read Lord of the Rings, the whole trilogy, and Shakespeare … So come 16, 17, I knew my English was good, I had topped it at school. But there was the social side and my personal side, which were fighting against that because it didn't seem to fit.

As I started getting into the Polynesian Panthers, I read a lot more in political books from Black Panthers: Malcolm X, and Angela Davies – a lot of it from the United States, California. I suddenly realised that this thing wasn't only happening here; I could relate to what was going on over there: the stark racism. I felt the same thing here.

Some of the activities that we got involved in to help our people were things like homework centres. At that time we were being sent to school then given homework to take home but no table or desk to work on. It was just unheard of. You come home; you help mum with the dishes or housework, or

a) 'Community Food Programme' *The People's Voice*. (Polynesian Panther Newspaper Articles Archive).
b) 'The Panther Movement Social ticket' 1971. (Etta Gillon [née Schmidt] archive).
c) Polynesian Panther Movement: Home-work Centre poster. (Will 'Ilolahia archive).
d) 'When the Police Come to Your Door...' poster, which accompanied the
Legal Aid Booklet. (Roger Fowler archive).

dad with whatever. But by then it would be too late. And then good night! 'What about my homework?' – 'Oh, you go to school to do your work.'

With the help of a schoolteacher, Bill Maung (a Buddhist priest from Western Springs College, formerly Seddon High School), we managed to get a city council building in Williamson Ave and had that as a homework centre for children that came from all over the place.

Lito: Sounds quite tame compared to the name Panthers. Were the Panthers ever in trouble with the law?

Tigi: Yes. We had a military wing directed by a minister of defence (I was minister [of] culture; I suppose it was because I wrote poetry and read books: they thought I was a nerd). When it came to certain issues like racist landlords who evicted people without notice while their living conditions were really bad, we would front up. To the landlord we would say: 'Fix this, fix that or else!' [Tigi gestures with his hands.] You know, like this. That seemed to be the only language they understood. Eventually, out of that came Tenants' Protection. At that time in Kingsland, Grey Lynn, a lot of Polynesian

Polynesian Panther demonstration on K'Rd protesting about the need for more public facilities for Polynesian youth in the city. (Nigel Bhana archive).

people were living in rental housing and they were being ripped off. So we tried to change attitudes; tried to educate them as to their rights.

Lito: So you got a little bit militant in trying to do that?

Tigi: In the end we ended up being militant and aggressive. When the Dawn Raids were happening, a lot of the people in Kingsland, Grey Lynn and Ponsonby had their doors kicked in at five o'clock in the morning … A group of us, including the military wing, got together with some cars and some Palagi students who had the cars; we went out to the Minister of Immigration's house. Three o'clock in the morning we were out there with loud hailers and spotlights and shone them on his house: 'Bill Birch, come out with your passport now!' When the lights went on and they all came out, we'd take off. Just to turn the tables; we knew where he lived.

So that was non-violent struggle and passive protest. At first those things worked but when they don't, then you have to try as many alternatives as you can. At that time there was a police investigation group: a task force, created solely to go around to Pacific Island areas like pubs in Otahuhu, Glen Innes and Ponsonby (The Gluepot). They were totally into aggravating people and enticing arrests for fighting and drunkenness. Whereas they didn't go around to other places where it was predominantly European and they were doing the same things. By then having cars and European friends with cars, we would follow the police around (The PIG patrol). Until then we were beating the feet; walking around a lot.

We also started printing out legal aid pamphlets that we were told about by our European political activists. David Lange was one of them helping us with that; any information that we needed we would ring him up or ask him for help. On Friday and Saturday nights we would go out to the pubs and talk to people. It was really hard then because we were young. A lot them (young and old) would say, 'Ahh, what do you want here? What legal aid?' And when I look at it now it was crazy; you don't go to places like that and not expect to have a fight. But we weren't acting as a gang, which was the thing then; when everybody wore patches in the pubs. We were out there trying to educate and help our people: what to do in certain situations and leaving phone numbers: 'Give us a ring if you are in trouble'.

Lito: That belief then led you, Tigi, to He Taua and the land march that Dame Whina Cooper won; the Springbok Tour; Bastion Point? You actually got arrested didn't you, for demonstrating?

'Street or dancehall? You choose'. (Nigel Bhana archive).

Tigi: Yep Bastion Point, 1978: I have still got my arresting papers. There were about 220 of us arrested at Bastion Point. I went as a Niuean because I know that what happens to the Māori people eventually will happen to us. If I look the other way then I'm not doing what I believe is right. You stand up for people that are oppressed because coming from a solo-parent family you sort of get that affinity with poor and oppressed people.

In my early reading of books I discovered that you have got to stay on the right side of history, and as a Niuean we have a lot to do with that because 'We can differentiate between right and wrong' – we know what is right; we have to do it. When the Springboks came along [in 1981] I wasn't going to stand for that: having any apartheid system being celebrated down here while I'm alive and well. That's an affront to any brown or black-skinned person.

So being in the Panthers as well, we did organise to protest and be involved. When it came to the crunch, be there at the front because things did start turning ugly. A lot of the pro-tour people antagonised a lot of ordinary folk who took up that right to protest. For being one of the hard nuts and being used to aggravation, I ended up being in the front. At the same time, being in a reggae band with singing songs like: 'Get up, stand up ...' I can't just sing and do nothing: I have to go all the ways.

I mean, look at what's happening right now: Mandela is free. So I know that I was on the right side of history then. But I'm glad and I give thanks that in New Zealand we can stand up and say, 'Yeah, we fought against that.' And even though I was one of the ones imprisoned for it, my loss is my loss; the time that I didn't spend with my family and stuff.

Like I remember my sister brought Ché up to Mount Eden prison to visit Dad while he was locked up. Not for any rape, burglary, theft or any of that, but for protesting against apartheid. Well, that's me as a Niuean. I didn't like it because he was that young and he didn't understand but now he knows … We were taught motu Palagi: it's a white country. Well the majority of it still is but the changes are happening and that's what I see. Maybe the inter-marriage bit; the mixing of races of people: that's a good sign; that's part of it. But still there's that hard-core. I don't see hard-core the other way; brown people totally wanting to be on their own and kick everybody else out … But I see it from the other way. Slowly it has to change; education is one way; inter-marriage and the raising of mixed children; all New Zealand; all form this country, Aotearoa.[3]

Indian Panther
NIGEL BHANA TALKS WITH WILL 'ILOLAHIA

In the beginning of the Polynesian Panthers, I was not a brother because I was an Asian. I didn't classify myself as an Asian living in Auckland, the biggest Polynesian population ever out. All my friends were Polynesians. Joining the Panthers was hard because in the first year I was never allowed to be a member. It was just Māori and other Polynesians. Until they recognised me, they took me on face value while being a person. And that's how I became a member of the Polynesian Panthers …

My biggest contribution to the Polynesian Panthers was when I was at Seddon Tech at the time … And we started up, myself and a fellow called David Maung … getting teachers involved on Ponsonby Road school teaching system: the homework centres at the Church (WEA). That was my first involvement and from there it gets bigger and bigger. And then we moved to Williamson Ave because there were so many people – we were getting kids all the way from Remuera … All of them were just coming to learn. Half of us couldn't read. We were just going through the school education system; going through the motions of doing things like that …

coming out of Paremoremo. Soon as they got out, they had nowhere to go. OK. Bang! Let's find them something: place, work, whatever. Give them some compassion so they're not lost.

Betty Wark was one of the main people in Ponsonby. So much respect for her because she actually lived in the same street as I did in Albany Road. And people used to come out of 'Pare' to her

---

Christchurch Star   June 1973

Relax. The Polynesian Panther Party is not a violent group like the image projected by the Black Panther movement in the United States

---

The second thing I was involved in was when the Panthers did a book of legal aid. This was a major thing because, at that time, I got away from the gang scene and legal aid; just telling everyone, young kids their rights …

The next part was the homeless, especially in Auckland. It was horrendous; setting up for people who didn't have places to go or live, or whatever. Trying to find places; not just a halfway house, but sort of set them up and then move them on. When Polynesian Panthers got their house behind the police station (Redmond St), we actually had people staying there full-time. A lot of people were coming out of prison, especially Māori men

house. Until the day she died, she had people that had done life and nowhere to go. Bang! Put them in.

Panthers and People's Union used to send a bus up every month. We didn't even know who we were going to visit. Get passes. Go up to 'Pare'.
Visit prisoners that had no-one. You didn't even know them. And just sit there. Rap away. Have a good time. Just talk to them and that. And when they come out of jail, they knew they had a home. They knew they had a whānau to go to, because a lot of them had nothing else at all.

Not just Paremoremo, but Waikeria was where my age group was; young offenders. We would go down to Waikeria to visit; take magazines, books, chocolates … whatever. And when a lot of these people got out of jail, they 'respected' it too.

The Panthers actually united a lot of gangs because the media in Auckland, at that stage, loved it … when Polynesians and Māori were fighting each other, they loved that sensation. And then the Panthers managed to get them together and say, 'Come on boys – why fight against each other? Gotta work together!' And that's when the legal aid book actually came out. It got them together. They had a home; they had everything.

Panthers actually got educational wise and inside your head. To educate you on the political aspects of what was going on, because we weren't naïve. We knew what was going down but the Panthers actually took it another step: 'Come on you fellas. This is what is happening.'

Auckland was the most racist place out. Especially against Polynesians, and this was the biggest Polynesian city in the world … The newspapers loved us just if we did anything wrong. The newspapers just loved anything that went 'down' …

As I said, it took nearly a year before they actually recognised me for my abilities. Because: 'Hello! Here's a little Indian Boy. What's an Indian Boy fighting for? Polynesian rights? Māori rights? And what's this little Indian Boy doing? He should be with his community and learn his culture and all that.' Which I had already done.

When I joined the Panthers, I was actually disowned by 90 per cent of my own family. Bar my parents. My parents stuck with me. That was one thing. As long as I was doing something, they didn't care. My house was always open. I used to have Samoans, Tongans, Raros. They used to sleep at home. While my parents used to feed them Indian food … Well, Asians, I was thinking – even today – still do not recognise the Polynesians … They were

second class citizens. Ninety per cent were classified as menial labourers and workers … They weren't seen as lawyers, accountants. Whereas Asians were: 'Hello. You have got to become a doctor. You have got to become a lawyer. You have got to become an accountant.' Things like that.

Before the Māori Land March started, the Panthers, especially with Ama [Rauhihi] and Tigi [Ness], with the People's Union started up a committee in Auckland … [We] had already been to Waitangi about four times. We were always up there for their support. All the time.

When the committee was formed, we went up north. I was thinking it was with Tame Iti, Syd Jackson, Te Tiphai, Lamm, Joe Hawke. All of us. We all went up there and we marched from up north all the way to Parliament. [We camped at Parliament after the march finished.] We stayed there because when the march finished we saw that: hello, it actually hasn't been resolved …

After that I actually went to Australia … Our closest neighbours we always used to fight with over Nelson Mandela all the way overseas; the Black Panthers in the United States. Australia was the most racist place I have ever experienced. And I was glad the Panthers sent me over. It was just an eye opener for the way Aborigines were treated …

Five women came to New Zealand, sponsored by the Panthers, in 1973. They came to see what was actually happening with Māori and other Polynesian cultures. And it was an eye-opening for them. They thought it was sweet: 'What are you fellas worried about? You fellas have got it easy compared to what they were actually doing over there.'

The social side of Ponsonby was into playing league, sports, having a good time. Not getting drunk or anything like that. And still getting motivated. And that's the thing the Panthers always had in their head. It was always political. It wasn't a nine-to-five job or whatever. People used to ring up the Panthers at 2 o'clock in the morning or someone's house and say: 'Excuse me. I'm down at the Central Police Station. Can you get me a lawyer? I need bail.' Things like that. So you're always doing something …

I met my wife, which is hard case. Been together for nearly 28 years now. And the way I actually met her was on a bus trip to Paremoremo. A bus trip to Paremoremo of all places to go to. Sitting next to her on a bus …

I think the biggest evil in Auckland at that stage was the police and the system itself. Because we were getting political and next minute there was drugs and everything coming on the scene. When drugs started coming on the scene, that's when they knew: hello, the same as they say, like, 'Polynesians – give them a bottle of beer. Boof! It's gone!'

Now these Polynesians were political, educated, whatever. We were going up to the university, doing seminars – whatever up there. Talking all the time. Albert Park. We were doing talks up there on a Sunday afternoon. I used to love Sunday afternoons because we could go up there and get onto the platform and try and educate all these Europeans that are going to university because they are going to be our next politicians or whatever. And try and tell them, 'Now this is what's going on, not just in Ponsonby but Grey Lynn, Otara, West Auckland and Mangere.'

And then after that – next minute they'll have six bands going. And then that's when the drugs started coming on the scene and the police didn't want to know it. Which I reckon was the downfall of a lot of political parties, especially the young ones. Because I'm sure that they infiltrated the drugs onto

the scene, because there were no convictions. There was no nothing.

South Auckland. We went there (I think it was early 1972) when the Stormtroopers had hit the headlines because they had smashed up Howick or Papatoetoe; had a massive brawl. And so we went out there to an area dominated by 90 per cent Māori: Where the Panthers were, was 90 per cent 'other' Polynesians.

And we took our legal aid books. Every Thursday and Friday we would go out on the streets of Otara giving out legal aid books. Stop. Talk to them; they'd look: phone numbers. Oh yes and a lot of response we did get back from these people, 'We need a lawyer or we need this. Mum's beating up Dad; we need food; we haven't got enough food.'

When the Polynesian Panthers and People's Union set up the food bank in Ponsonby itself, I think it was one of the first food banks apart from the Salvation Army and Red Cross. But how many Polynesians are going to go to the Red Cross? 'Oh, can I have some food?' 'Go to your own people.' 'Not a problem.'

There's no whakamā – no shyness with our food bank. Because if you are hungry, you gotta put food on your table. It was there. And that's what the Polynesian Panthers and the People's Union actually did. Roger Fowler set that up.

We were lucky we were getting it from the markets. Which I think they weren't allowed to do because it [meant] cutting out the grocers and supermarkets. They would rather dump it than give it away to people. That was where the food was going; taking it to the dump.

Even from the time we left from up north to the time we got to Wellington [on the Māori Land March], I don't know how to describe it. There was so much racism. Especially from white people saying, 'What are you fighting for? You get the dole. You get this. We give you that. We have given you handouts.' But they didn't realise what the march was about. People were fighting for their own land. This is our own land. We want it back! And wherever we went we got racist comments – abuse – people wanted to punch our heads in, and stuff like that. And we told this the whole time we were on the march. We never went into a pub. We were lucky; 99 per cent of the places we stayed at were marae. These people had to welcome us on. Feed us. Sleep. It was good. But as soon as we started walking again, the abuse that we got from people was unreal.

That was one thing that was hard case on the march. Because the perception was that Māori and other Polynesians never got on. And that's the deal as Pākehā. But on the march we were 'as one' … There were so many groups – Ngā Tamatoa, Panthers, People's Union, civil liberties, communists, whatever. And everyone was united.

That was another thing: I think a lot of New Zealanders did not like it because, hello: a Māori was walking with a Polynesian and a Pākehā next to him. 'What's going on here? What's going on here! This is not way the system is meant to be; these fellows should be in the headlines, "Mongrel Mob, Black Power fighting each other. Head Hunters and Nigs fighting each other."'

That's the thing, a lot of people even in my younger days like with the Junior Nigs and the Black Panthers, before the Polynesian Panthers started: there was no such thing as that. We never actually went out looking for violence or anything like that. Everyone knew who was in Ponsonby, who was in Henderson, who was in Otara. It wasn't Māori against Polynesian or anything like that.

Oh yes. Oh yes. It's changed my attitude. Like I work in the hospitality industry, selling alcohol that the Panthers don't actually agree with: all the drugs and that. And I have been serving it up for years. But now I can go into local hotels where there are young gang members, and I can still talk to them and say, 'OK. Come on, you fellas. You have had enough.' Or things like that. I can actually relate to them from those early days of the Panthers. Knowledge and that. And I still tell them: 'OK, so and so is in trouble. OK, I will get you a lawyer.'

So and so will say, 'I need a house or halfway house to go to.' I can actually find places. I still have so many contacts in my situation. I can still do that. And without the Panthers I would not have that 'Knowledge'. I would never have that knowledge because I would have gone: 'God! Look at that dumb nigger over there.' And that's what they used to call us – 'niggers'. And that's how we became the Junior Nigs …

West Auckland was growing up as young Māori. More Māori than other Polynesians stayed out that way. They actually only had one nightclub. But then the local 'shopping community', I don't know what they called themselves, decided, 'OK. We are going to shut this place down because it is congregating with heaps of Māori, Polynesians and that.' So they closed it down and the Panthers tried to get it reopened, which never happened.

The Youth Centre. It was actually a centre for Māori in that area. So when they closed it down, the Head Hunters started up again and they are still going now. And the police are so scared of them. Yes. Ha ha ha ha. That's when the Head Hunters started up after that, because there was nowhere else for them to go.

What I didn't want to say was that some of our guys smashed the whole shopping centre over.

Yes, that was the military wing of the Panthers.

And that was another thing. The Junior Panthers did a lot of security work for Church groups, for their socials. And because they didn't pay for security guards, they were usually the same age as the people going into the premises. They could relate to them; they weren't going to stand over and say, 'Take off your leather jacket!' and all that type of stuff. 'Go in. Enjoy yourself. Have a good time. Make sure you get home safely.' That was like Reverend Beck's on Jervois Rd.

Another that helped out the Panthers was a fellow called Rick Grymes. He ended up doing the PD Centre in Parnell. And he took care of quite a few of the youth in Ponsonby who were in a big gang group associated with the Panthers: the Apaches. He took on a young fellow called Robert Brown; showed him the ropes. Stuff like that.

Another lady in Ponsonby was Auntie Hope. She was one of my idols. Her house was open 24 hours a day for anyone; regardless of Polynesian or Māori.

Landlords were just unreal. Fighting landlords; in the end they would always win. People's rights; a lot of Māori people and other Polynesians didn't know their rights. They're getting charged exorbitant rents. If the landlord knew he was going to sell the place a month later: 'Hello. Your rent's going up.' 'But we only got this much money in our hand. How are we going to pay the rent?' Things like that.

The Tenants' Aid Brigade had lawyers involved with the Panthers; we referred people that rang up; give them to the Tenants' Brigade. They would then deal with all the issues; they knew all the ins and outs, the law. The whole lot. Which a lot of us younger ones didn't know but we still knew our rights: 'Hello. You can't do this!' Landlords, trying to evict people.

There was a vision of a lot of landlords that we knew: 'Hello. Sorry you Polynesian people. We are gonna move you all out of Ponsonby. Move you further along.' And they actually started doing that in early 1975 with a lot of the associates of the Panthers – the Apaches in Ponsonby. They lived in Georgina St, down off College Hill. They had houses and stayed in there for years and years.

And next minute the landlords were saying, 'OK. We gotta a new subdivision out in Henderson; a brand new house and everything, and started moving them … And just one by one, everyone was starting to get moved out of Ponsonby …

It's called Spot the Nigger! … And one thing I'll say is: growing up in Ponsonby, and at least with the Polynesian Panthers, the streets were safe! You could walk the streets of Ponsonby; go down to Queen Street, K Road and never get molested; never get robbed. Never gonna get attacked. Now these days, you can't even walk the streets and you can't say it's a Māori or other Polynesian and that.

Without the Panthers in the early days, a lot of the youth in Ponsonby, Grey Lynn, Point Chev and especially in those areas getting into West Auckland would have ended up as gangsters. We started to get politically aware and that's what kept us away from putting that stupid patch on our back. What is a patch on your back? The only patches we had on our backs was our league jerseys and to be proud to be a Panther. And to help not just us get politically wise, but our parents, because a lot of parents didn't comprehend what was going down – how we were getting victimised; ripped off by the system. Shit like that. Plus the next generation coming along too. I think that actually saved us.

Ninety per cent of all kids with Panther parents have actually gone a long way because they get that awareness from their parent, which you wouldn't

Polynesian Panthers; from left to right, back row: Theresa Ahmu, Etta Schmidt, Henry Neenee, Eddie Williams. Front row: Rosie Sanft, Sam Vete, Nooroa Teavae. (Etta Gillon [née Schmidt] photo archive).

have if you grew up in a house full of gangsters. Whatever!

All you know is: 'Hello. That's going to be it, rob, beat … whatever.' And that was the concept of the Pākehās, and the Europeans. That was their concept. But as kids, the next generation, seeing their parents get politically wise, gets them politically wise.

And the next best thing after the Panthers was reggae. When Herbs came along and a lot of other reggae bands, they actually made the young kids really aware of what was going on but not Bob Marley, although fair enough, he was the founder of

it. The Panthers also had a lot of involvement with Herbs and Bastion Point.

Ronald was first printed between Ngā Tamatoa, Polynesian Panthers and the People's Union. And as far as I know, it was the first political Polynesian – Māori magazine that came out. Communist magazines were always out. And People's Union came out later. But *Ronald* was the first that gave awareness to a lot of young Māori and other Polynesians; my generation. And it united them.

And they could relate to it because it was very easy reading; it wasn't complicated and it had a lot of heart. There was honesty in it and that was before the *Panther's Rapp* …

With the Polynesian Panthers at the house in Redmond Street, it was like an office; a halfway house. We had people staying there: myself, Zac Wallace's missus, her name was Vicki; her two kids were three and four, might even be a bit younger; and my wife.

To have showers we used to go out in the car park where we had hooked up cold showers with a cold tap. This was in the early hours of the morning between five and half past six, before cars were driving past.

At that stage in Ponsonby, there were a couple of supermarkets where we knew exactly when they were going to get deliveries; bread and milk. The bread-man, he was choice. I think it was Tip Top bread. We only took what we needed, two loaves of bread and a couple of punnets of doughnuts. And in the end, he used to put those on top of the trays for us. Thank you, Tip Top. Thank you, Tip Top bread …

In the early days, the senior members of the Panthers were students. The junior members were all unemployed. We didn't rip off the system. None of us were on the dole or anything like that. So we actually had to rely on our families to support us for anything, food-wise, clothing, whatever. And that's why we always walked the streets. But we never got hungry, because we always had a house to go to and have a feed …

In joining the Panthers, I did have a problem with the senior members because of my ethnic origin. But in the end it didn't really matter. It just didn't matter. It just boiled down to: 'Hello! Hey this is an Indian but he's a Polynesian!' And what we were classified as, didn't matter. As I said, whether Māori or Polynesians, we were one. Simple as that.

It wasn't a gang thing or the prospect, like material stuff. We shared as a whānau thing because of what we had. If I had a cigarette and you knew it was being smoked – puff. We shared it around. Even if we did go to hotels or whatever. Or go for a meal, if we had enough money for two plates and there's eight of us, we shared it all. We shared the whole lot and that's where the whānau stuff came in. And that is part of Polynesian culture … Asians or Indians even say I am an Indian person. I don't classify myself as an 'Asian'. In those days I thought I was a Polynesian anyhow because I grew up with the aroha inside my heart …

My Experience in the Polynesian Panthers
ETTA GILLON (NÉE SCHMIDT)

This I dedicate to my brother Fred.

My earliest memory of the Polynesian Panthers was through my brother Fred Schmidt, who is now deceased. It was thanks to my brother Fred that I became involved with the group.

I was at the initial meeting of the formation of the Polynesian Panthers. I found it daunting and possibly a bit intimidating as I knew that some of my brother's friends, I deemed at that time, were misbehaved, renowned troublemakers or worse. My brother and his mates appeared to be enthusiastic and keen to embark on this new venture. The gathering was for the purpose of forming a group for the benefit of the Polynesian people – our people, not necessarily just for the FOBs (Fresh off the Boat) or individual races like the Samoans, Tongans,

Niuean, Fijians, Māori and so on, but for the needy and all immigrants of the Pacific basin. That is, culturally as one.

The group felt the need was also there to help within the community as a whole; for them to be identified as part of a crucial entity; to help our own. I thought this was the start of something positive. I also knew that if my father was to have seen the large gathering at home (unruly gangs were rife at the time), he would be very upset and kick everyone out. Sure enough one day when my father arrived home early from work, out the lot went: jumping out the windows; scooting out the side doors; every which way they scampered. Thank goodness we had a big home then, as I am sure my dad would not know how to cope if he was in a confrontational arena.

Eventually, my brother Fred became one of the foundation members of the Polynesian Panthers and was known as the front person or communications officer. To his mates he was called 'The Captain'.

My first introduction to all the proposed members at that time was at a gathering organised with the local pastor at the Baptist Church and some of the foundation members of the Polynesian Panthers. Some of the girls and boys I knew from school: my cousin Eddie, my neighbour and friend Melani, and a few of my brother's mates. Fred introduced me and my friends to the group. He was protective of us, but assured us that all his mates were to be trusted. Later on, they became our 'soul brothers'. He also knew that as a whole, we would bring some positive input to the Panthers, and so, later on, we helped formulate a constitution and by-law that we all knew needed to be put into place. We felt we were there for a real purpose and for something really good.

Those were exciting times. For a few of us girls, our exposure to racism before meeting the group was limited. However, once we met a mixture of young, interesting, vibrant, culturally sensitive young people in our newly formed group, we felt enriched by their care and attitude to life.

The oppression experienced by some of the Panthers was an eye-opener to me and with it, made me feel quite inadequate. I suppose I knew then that I needed to take a much-needed will to fight and stand up for my rights and the rights of others. We believed in equality for all (Pacific Islanders included), while identifying and showing empathy with our American counterparts and their struggle. While growing up in New Zealand, we opposed apartheid and with it, the total opposition to any ties with South Africa, including sport.

There was great pride in being a Panther and wearing the appropriate garb. We stood out, looked the part (loved the berets) and, I suppose, looked quite intimidating to those who knew us and what we stood for. Because of my nursing experience, I soon became the medical adviser and felt that if there were any medical issues affecting people in our area, I would be there to assist with the appropriate information. From memory, at that time hunger and malnutrition among the very young and the elderly were very real, sad issues, especially among those who lived on their own.

We helped to run food co-ops and, with the local Baptist minister, we established two home-work centres. We knew that education would be the key to help fellow Pacific Islanders to integrate into the New Zealand way of life.

To also assist the cause, we fundraised for different projects in the area. Our main office was like a drop-in centre; a focal point for all members to gather and vent any problems and/or address any Pacific Island issues.

We endeavoured to ensure that people in the community were made aware of their rights and/or assist them in any way possible. Whether Polynesian, Māori, European, Palagi, young or old, we were always there for them. The elderly were assisted with their shopping, chores, and trips to events and tourist sites around Auckland. The youth were helped with their homework and any other problems they may have encountered or felt

These two images are of People's Union Co-op food store and Ponsonby Community Food programmes in 1977. The Polynesian Panthers worked with the People's Union to alleviate the hardship suffered by Pacific peoples and others in Ponsonby because of inflated food costs. (Roger Fowler archive).

that needed to be addressed.

We were there to protest against the Vietnam War, apartheid or any other forms of inequality. It made us feel so proud to be part of the group and all that it stood for. We were aware that the up-and-coming youth in the area were watching us. So our aim was to become good role models for them. This was mainly to ensure that our hard efforts would not be in vain and that the younger members of our group would carry on and strive for what we believed in.

I believe we worked well as a team. We believed in ourselves and succeeded to help wherever; we achieved so much in the short time I was there. Unfortunately, my nursing studies kept me from assisting further. Our hearts, aspirations and memories in 'Little Polynesia' will always be there, and I would like to believe that we as a group made a much-needed positive contribution to all concerned.

It is thanks to my brother Fred and our 'soul' brothers and sisters of the PPM, that our efforts were at the forefront, reaching great heights of recognition.

The richness and diversity of our cultures have been realised. We should be proud of the positive achievements that we have all made in our own way. As for me, I have come full circle and I am honoured to have been part of the Polynesian Panther group. With me now, teaching English to foreign students and adults I find quite fulfilling, as I know it helps them to integrate into a new life; the New Zealand way of life. They too can enrich us all with their cultures, as they reach their full potential.

Fa'afetai lava!! **Be proud!!** *Alofa, kia kaha!! Malo e lelei!*

STRIDE FORWARD SON OF SAFOTU

Sunrise, sunset, sunrise, sunset
Frangipani, hibiscus and singing
Stride forward young man of Safotu
Savaii, bananas, palusami, fish, taro
Sweet succulent juicy cocoa beans
Gone still, but not forgotten
Stride forward old man of valima
Welcome, welcome son of Safotu
Volcano, lava rocks, coconut trees sway
Nothing has changed but look at you
You in your sophisticated palagi ways
Sunrise, sunset: why do these words haunt me
Day in sunrise, day out sunset
Yes! The years have faded for valima
Now, here I am, I have buried so much
Sadness like dreaded goose bumps
Treading over my naked shoulders
My heart wrenched out and wrung out every
Drop of aching strand. The hurt so great
Why, why did he pass away?
He is my only hope of survival
My sheer existence shattered
Who do I turn to now?
Sunrise, sunset, Falavalava

This memory of despair so vivid
The loss yes! Oh! So great
Like a great wave rushes the emotion
Is so overwhelming
I know that life changes
And that your end was in sight
You were the love of my life
My everything, my father
And at that time, to me, my only family

It is the here, over your grave I stand
The here, that I feel that the pain was
so excruciating
And the now, that with me I bring my
beloved family
To share the love and warmth within my
homeland
To feel your love which enveloped me
Oh those so many years ago
Sunrise, sunset
I Thank You. I Thank You
You son of Safotu

Recollections of a Panther minister for youth

VINCENT TUISAMOA

My mother, Agnes, first took me up to the Panther's HQ at Redmond Street in 1974. First up, I stayed out on the porch while a meeting was going on inside. It was with the Panthers and the 'J' Team set up by the city council to target problems with inner city youth. It usually involved visiting schools.

The Panthers were also active in anger-management projects: the Black Men's (and Black Women's) Workshop, a joint project with Whakahau. Lagi and Grace were friends who were involved with its activities. Other people who actively participated were Tony Fonoti, John and Jake Matafeo, Brian Lepo with Zena (Kōhanga Reo – Hilary College). One of the methods to convey the message was with 'situational skits'. There was one about an island boy going out with a Palagi girl – crossing the racial divide. It was also about the first instances of going 'PC' – not calling girls 'chicks': I told off my boys for calling them that: 'Don't belittle. Once you start doing that you start belittling society itself.'

A non-sexist stance; to broaden perspectives on sexism held by young kids, especially Polynesians. That's what was needed – not 'Hey nigger! Hey bitch, get your eagle on with me – but something like the words of Scribe, Che Fu, Nesian Mystic, and some members of the Polynesian Panthers, and especially their children who are carrying the legacy of their forebears: 'Be proud of who you are and not who you think you are.' It's about having a positive view; view with respect. I still think as a Panther, the ideology is still with me. I'm still trying to pass these ideals onto younger generations. Things like taking responsibility for your actions, like staying around for their pregnant partners.

The Panthers taught me how to avoid direct conflicts, how to read situations.

There is a picture within a picture. You don't go for the guy who is the loudest; look for whoever is pulling the strings. You got to look out for the sleeper. We also educated our youth on how to deal with harassment by the police: 'Are we being arrested? On what charge?' You give your name or address and that's all you gave once you were arrested. This was very important for some of our senior members in pubs; the Police Task Force was targeting them because of what I thought of as an abuse of power by political forces beyond them. The squad's brief was supposed to be policing violence and throwing out under-age drinkers.

As a result of this harassment, our people were too scared or too drunk to face this squad head-on, so the Panthers formed their own kind of 'Pig Patrol' with the help of some patrons and bar managers. There was a route that the Task Force followed: it usually looped around starting from the South Pacific (Snake Pit), Empire Hotel, to the Oxford, Suffolk, Gluepot, Star Hotel, Rising Sun, Family Naval, Kings Arms or the Astor, New Caledonia, Edinburgh Castle and then back to downtown. Isn't it interesting that the pubs that were visited were Polynesian waterholes but not to the extent of the Prospect in Howick or the White Horse in Pakuranga? Anyway, as soon as the police left one pub, someone would telephone or ride ahead.

Members of People's Union and Citizens Association for Racial Equality (CARE), also helped the Panthers to form Police Investigation Groups and so the PIG Patrol became better organised. Because of our lack of transport resources, we relied heavily on them for mobility. When the 'Waewae Express' got tired or the old 'Rubber Tyre Jandal' didn't have top gear, we would call up Roger Fowler and Lyn Doherty with their blue Combi van. I'm not sure but I think even Sione Lolly and Tim Shadbolt provided their old dungers and rust buckets. Much love and thanks to them and others for all their support. Some of the members also had access to the police radio frequency. But Pigs got wise to that and one time the paddy wagon did a U-turn and rammed what they thought was the monitoring vehicle. In that case it turned out to be just an ordinary citizen's car.

The sole purpose of the Panthers was to provide a voice for our Polynesian people, and not just with the heavy cost of and to lawyers sometimes volunteering on our behalf. No one else could take up the challenge: to walk the street, even if it meant the disapproval of a lot of our elders who kept their heads down. But, respectfully, it is in their nature as new immigrants to avoid confrontation. Their focus was to provide for their children; to sacrifice for a better life for all of us.

If you asked me whether I would revamp the Panthers, the answer is 'no'. We would be fighting the same fight as back then. We would be challenging the same 'interpreters': those opportunists who are seeking personal gain through the misfortune of our people. And the saddest thing of all is that these interpreters themselves are Polynesians. At least in those days, a racist was up front and in your face, in contrast to today, when they hide behind political correctness.

When the Dawn Raids and pursuit of Polynesian overstayers were at their height, the Panthers were an 'issue' so we were being 'watched'. You could tell if the phone was bugged by the double click when you picked up, or an echo in the background. We used to have codes set up for times like when Joe busted out of jail. When he rang me, I said, 'I'll be up there in half an hour.' It only took me five minutes but by the time I got back home, the Armed Defenders Squad had already visited. The rule on the street was clear: 'The police got tired of chasing you but never got tired of tracking you.'

We were fortunate to have a few allies in the newspaper media: John Minto, (Sione Lolly) through the *New Zealand Herald*, and John Hart for *West End News*. Our educational material, the *Panthers' Rap*. But the general media still had the better of us: Pacific Islanders were still made to look bad; that fear factor: 'Just because you are an Islander'. There was an instance of a group of sixth formers going on a 'horror tour' of K Road; they were told it was too dangerous to walk around after 11 pm. Even some of the rural Māori bros had certain perceptions of Polynesians in the city: 'Bunga, Bunga, Bunga'. All they could see was what the pro-establishment, granny-*Herald* was writing up. It was always spoken in a loving way, with aroha, but it just shows how Pacific Islanders have been demonised by the media and certain politicians, to the general public. The Panthers had an uphill mission in trying to change these cartoon images of big 'juju' lips, fuzzy hair, *lavalava*, jandals and 'no future' prospects – Muldoon and 'New Zealand the way you want it'.

David Lange, Panthers' legal adviser 1971–1976
WILL 'ILOLAHIA TALKS WITH DAVID LANGE

Will: David, as our legal adviser for the Polynesian Panthers from a period of 1971 till about '76 … give us your reflections of that period of time and … the group.

David: Most of my work with the Panthers was in Auckland, and there were certain characteristics of my clients which were common. They were youthful; they were not engaged in what they regarded as meaningful employment, or any sort of employment for that matter. And they also had problems in adjustments.

Many of them lived in families whose expectations of them was that they would behave in an urban environment in an alien country, in which many of them had been born, as if they were still in a village in a Pacific paradise; and the demands of Church conformity and the sheer time involved in being disciplined as with the expectation of parents was beyond many of them. It was in a time when you were starting to see an Auckland, the growth of clubs and night spots and drinking places and the city was taking on a sort of neon-light image, and this added to the possibilities of mayhem. The other interesting thing was that very seldom they get into trouble by themselves. They tended to do it in … twos or threes and twos or threes or fours. It was … easy for them then to become united in their non-conformity against the customs of the time.

The word 'gang' is wrong … in the criminology literature, a gang had at its very essence the determination of the members were bound together to further illegal activity. This was not the core of their activity, they were bound together in some sort of comradeship or exuberance or rebellion but it wasn't that they were professional criminals. They were behavioural malcontents who didn't conform to what a rather rough police system thought should be; and fairly common in the pattern of the work that I did was the very big cultural divide between policing and the young. The police were, one can understand … very hard-handed with a young Samoan and perhaps somewhat cautious of a well-dressed Pākehā that had had too much to drink after work. And there were clear differences in the way in which people were treated by police and the severity of it. But from my point of view the good thing was that the police were casual, too, about the gathering evidence on preparation of charges …

But there was one common thing was that they had no one to turn to except their comradeship within the Panthers and no one else was going to help them, no one else knew how to help them. They didn't have anyone … to turn to. And in fact, in many cases, parents didn't want to be involved. The sheer odium of turning up to a court was rather too much for them, they didn't want to know about it. So they performed pretty well by their duties of their peers in the Panthers. Many of them were quite engaging characters, but some of them

weren't … likely to recover from their experiences.

Will: Dave, I will always remember this thing about the charge of 'Idle and Disorderly', and I think you made this charge quite famous … I think there were, according to our records, 75 people who were charged with I & D. You seemed to have got all of them off. But you had this definition in regard to a bone I think. Could you explain that Dave because I think that was one of the major things that we quite admired about you … your ability to focus on the technicalities of charges.

David: Right. You see … I was operating under law which … had been unchanged in medieval tenses laws. It had been put into legislation. But the offences were casual stuff, behavioural offences and the charges had phrases which had gone out from the days of travelling tankers and they didn't work any more, but the police had never got used to the idea that they had to really do something. And so I could always get someone they used to charge with being Idle and Disorderly with insufficient law for me to support. But that was very easy to do because being Idle and Disorderly had nothing to do with the charge. I mean there was no doubt at all that most [of] my clients were Idle and Disorderly [laughs]. You can stop there and say that's it for them, right? But then the qualifications rule had no law for me to support.

Will: What was your major impressions of the group, the Panthers and what they were doing in regard to that period of time?

David: You've always got a problem with dealing with the law because you've got to accept that the law is a very deficient instrument of social change and goodness … it is not that I defended many people on charges where they were not guilty and I got a perfectly good legal result, I just didn't get the right result. The right result in fact was in conflict sometimes with what should be done. If only there'd been a halfway house where I could've said to someone, 'Hey look, I can defend you on this and get you off, but I'd like to be able to say that you should be helped. You should, without having a stain on your character or a conviction to your name, be given assistance under the guise of a course of training.' A sort of equivalent probation without the stigma of conviction … and the law never did that. It was always in my view deficient, and the Polynesian Panthers were able to bridge that gap because they would contest the legal aspect of it but then they would provide support and network to try to help that person keep out of the trouble that they'd fallen into.

The Panthers provided some substance to the possibility that there was an alternative to endless court appearances. There was as well as that, the downside, which was that some kids would've felt in power by having won. You know, getting off, and that's not always good for kids.

In co-operation with the Panthers we produced a set of notes [legal aid book] to provide some guide to young people about dealing with the police and what their rights were. Technically the book … was absolutely correct. Oh, absolutely correct, it was a statement of the law and it was very useful to some … assertion of their rights. On the other hand, when you have a culture in the police which was highly resentful of challenge to authority and was deeply aggrieved by people suggesting that some process or other had [not] been properly honoured by the police or that they weren't required to give them more than your name and address, you had the makings of a stoush in terms of some rearrests and overnighters in cells and in court the next morning … [In] the cultural clime, it could harm a young person as well as help

them and one of the things that has happened over the years is that degree of instant antipathy to insisting on process has faded in the police …

Will: So in some ways there was some sort of effect on the actual police state … or the system after they realised that what they were trained at in the police schooling was actually different than what was actually, technically, the law?

David: I think the police certainly became aware of their limitations in dealing with minority groups of whom the Polynesian Panthers was one. And they went to considerable lengths to deal with that. There has been in major cities a conspicuous improvement in … the manner of policing so that you no longer have instant alienation once you see someone who's a Samoan, for instance, on the street. It's become a function of change over the years in population trends as well. It has become now of course commonplace for Pacific Island police officers to be on the police force, Māori officers to be given positions of authority in the police force, and there is not the immediate identification of young Polynesians as a group which must be opposed to the police because some of the police are like them. So there is now a more practical view of the totality of the community when it comes to police.

Will: Dave, do you think the group was effective in those days, and has it made any significant contribution to New Zealand's society … as we know it today?

David: It was effective in a couple of ways. First of all, at the time when the legal aid system was appalling and when you didn't get much to do with anything, there was always an assurance that someone from the Panthers would get you a lawyer – that was a great benefit. Second thing was it had an approach to society-building and status-building merely by members within the Panthers and by working with it. So quite significant community leadership persistence, outside of the traditional lines of status in Pacific communities, came about through involvement in the Panthers. The old Samoan, Tongan practices of being respected because your father was X and you became Y, faded and the son of Z could become Mr A and that was a big difference. And that I think … gave young people the chance to see a future for themselves in a society which they were growing accustomed to against the background of families who were actually just approving of such big-headedness. So that break was necessary because, notwithstanding whatever the goodwill and intention of the parents were, many of them could not be savvy to a view of what it meant to be in a different country in the 20th century bringing up children. The [thing that] held back many of the people in Pacific communities in an extraordinary way was the Church. The rigours of money-giving and time-devotion and conformity to patterns of behaviour which were highly appropriate for village life just didn't work in Ponsonby.

Will: Well, one of the things that you … certainly changed for us Panthers, David, were our impressions or feelings about politicians. I'm not quite sure if you remember but when you stood for Mangere at the time, you were the only politician that we actually had a big riff in the group about – when we decided to come and help you canvas the community by doing all your leaflets and that kind of stuff. But you know that was a major thing for us in the sense that you changed our feeling about working within the system.

David: Yes well that's what they did. The Panthers became not pussycats but they became able to be inclusive. They were not some sect devoted to the paramountcy of ethnicity or determination to be different …

Will: Were there good times for you, Dave?

David: Oh they were good times, they were exciting times. As a young lawyer it was a time of exuberance, getting on, challenging …

There were parts of it that weren't good because if you were guilty and sometimes it was necessary, you paid for it. You couldn't be completely certain that the probation service was, in those days, ethnically diverse enough to cope with the young Polynesian clients …

For the Pacific people of today in New Zealand [the issue is] becoming educated. I am dependent on a Niuean nurse, a top-rate dialysis nurse who is highly skilled, looks after me well. The same is true for the medical practice and nurses, their level of confidence is accelerating all the time, and I stayed in South Auckland because I was born here, it's part of me and I grew up in it … All the joy of Pacific vitality and vibrancy of the different cultures all in a very narrow compass and so much more exciting than living in Remuera. So I live here and I think that Pākehā people are viewing Pacific people somewhat differently today. One of the problems with that is that they are now moving a little to prefer them to Māori and that's always a risk. I think the recent problems over the foreshore and seabed have tended to escalate the difference if you put into contrast these notions of Māori grief and threats [while] Pākehā feel no threat at all from Pacific aspiration and that's going to have to settle down. The Pākehā view of the so-called Māori struggle is a very mixed bag.

It always takes a few extremists to shift the centre of gravity, and I think they've done that and now it's time to pull their heads in [laughs] and we'd be better off as a result. The Pacific people are well regarded because of their warmth, because they mow the lawns and because they're quite good neighbours. Something which is really hard for people who don't live with Pacific people to understand. They have these stereotypical images of chaos and incompetence yet they always embarrass me when my lawn was always longer than theirs [laughs] and their kids were always ... well presented. Something which people now accept is being a norm and it's a silly way to judge people but there is a certain happiness for coexistence and as Pacific communities become more at ease in the European culture. The marginalisation which used to occur will fall off, and there will be a common cause between us all.

'United we stand, divided we fall' Polynesian Panther Party poster celebrating close ties between Pacific and tangata whenua as 'Polynesians'. (Will 'Ilolahia archive).

Working in partnership
ROBERT LUDBROOKE

The 1970s saw a coming together of four separate movements that sought solutions to the disadvantages encountered by Māori and Pacific peoples under the monocultural justice system of Aotearoa New Zealand. This partnership sought to address the social injustice and racism, imposed on the largest Polynesian community on the Pacific Rim. The idea of 'cultural diversity' in such times of post-colonialism and ethnic intolerance was inconceivable.

The four movements were:

1. A strong Ponsonby Community Association represented by a mix of Māori community workers and activists (such as Betty Wark, Fred Ellis, Eddie McLeod, Anna Jones), people from the Pacific Islands (Coral Lavulavu) and Pākehā/Palagi.

2. Māori and Pacific activist organisations Ngā Tamatoa and Polynesian Panthers.

3. 'white on white' Pākehā activists under the umbrella of the Auckland Committee on Racism and Discrimination (ACORD), which had a number of Māori and Pacific advisers (such as Syd Jackson and Will 'Ilolahia) and which pressed strongly the concept of institutional racism, which meant that the institutions in Aotearoa New Zealand reflected the values and attitudes of the Pākehā majority thus creating injustice to Māori and Pacific peoples

4. A small group of lawyers including Piers Davies who were working for change within the legal profession and the legal system in [an] attempt to raise the consciousness of lawyers and to set in place means of redressing the injustices suffered by non-Pākehā as a result of the institutional racism that characterised the justice system at that time.

While there were no formal links between these different groups, there was regular contact between them. In addition, a lot of people concerned about racism and discrimination attended annual hui held by the Race Relations Council.

Among their activities, Ngā Tamatoa and Polynesian Panthers provided practical support for Māori and Pacific peoples caught up in the criminal courts. They liaised with sympathetic lawyers to get specialist legal help.

Efforts by all of these movements resulted in some important innovations in legal services. For example, a duty solicitor scheme introduced in 1973 gave every person appearing before the court access to specialist legal advice at the time of their first appearance.

The need for a comprehensive legal service in areas with a large concentration of Māori and Pacific peoples became obvious when the Community Advice Bureau in Ponsonby, Glen Innes, Queen St, Avondale and Otara discovered it was difficult to find lawyers to accept referrals. The main barriers were the lack of law firms in these localities and sufficient lawyers to take on criminal, debt and family law cases. There was also concern that many lawyers had little understanding of tikanga Māori, fa'asamoa and other Pacific cultures.

The Grey Lynn Neighbourhood Law Office (NLO) was established in 1977 in response to such concerns. It was a collaboration between the local Māori and Pacific communities and Palagi lawyers, including myself and Piers Davies. It provided a warmer and more accessible version of advocacy law for communities in the lower socio-economic groups, predominantly Māori and other Polynesians, of New Zealand society.

In its first two years, the NLO went out to meet Church leaders and other influential people in the Māori and Pacific communities in Ponsonby and Grey Lynn. Māori and Pacific peoples were also strongly represented on its management committee. The NLO received referrals from a wide range of community groups including Polynesian Panthers court officers. Will 'Ilolahia was a strong supporter of the NLO in those early years.

The original intention was that no fees would be charged to clients. However, the NLO was severely under-resourced, making it necessary to ask clients for a modest financial contribution. This practice has continued.

Acknowledgments: My thanks to Piers Davies for his input in the preparation of this document. This article draws on Robert Ludbrooke's work in progress, celebrating 25 years of Community Legal Service, the Grey Lynn Neighbourhood Law Office.

Civil rights and PIG patrols
ROGER FOWLER, COORDINATOR OF THE PONSONBY PEOPLE'S UNION (1971–1979)

The People's Union for Survival and Freedom was set up in Ponsonby/Grey Lynn in 1971, mainly by young radicals who had been involved in the protest movement against the Vietnam War. Many had studied articles and books by leaders of the United States Black Panther Party, and related to their staunch stand against oppression and for self-determination by organising their own grass-roots communities for their own survival and self-defence, and solidarity networks known as 'revolutionary inter-communalism'. The Black

Panther Party presented new leadership in the struggle around real, urgent issues facing their communities – poverty, poor housing, sub-standard health and education, police brutality, etc. While many in the anti-war movement talked about 'learning from the Vietnamese resistance' and 'bringing the War back home' Huey Newton and the Black panthers were doing it by empowering their communities to stand up and fight back. Their community programmes sustained and strengthened their united purpose. They were fighting for survival and liberty.

Panther Rapp   February 1975

The P.I.G. Patrol

The members of the People's Union were multicultural, though mainly young inner-city Pākehā and Māori working people and students. We set up an office in an old shop in Ponsonby Road, compiled a 'Ten Point Statement of Direction' based around demands for community control of police, housing, education, work and nutrition, and against exploitation. The popular Food Co-op became the organising vehicle of community protests and pickets. We held several meetings with the Polynesian Panther Movement (PPM) and quickly established a common bond based on a shared vision of community control and resistance to oppression and exploitation.

Members of both groups worked together, in particular around the People's Union Food Co-op and the Visitors' Bus Services to Paremoremo and Waikeria, and supporting various struggles against evictions, shoddy housing and police harassment. We also assisted with the production of some of the Panther Party leaflets and 'Panther Raps' newspaper.

During the Muldoon years police intimidation continued in other ways, with the racist bullying tactics of the newly formed Police Task Force, which travelled in large convoys of paddy wagons and staged heavy-handed displays of force. We worked closely with the Panthers and CARE (Citizens Association for Racial Equality). The Police Investigation Group (PIG) patrols were formed because of the Police Task Force. Convoys of police paddy wagons and cars would descend mainly on bars in great numbers and would provoke people into situations. They picked on bars frequented by PIs and Māori and 70 per cent of arrests were PIs. There was distaste in the community.

Groups got together and would follow the police and hand out leaflets. The media got involved so it became controversial. It was a very ugly situation. They caused it. One or two smart comments and things would start.

We published a list of civil rights and what you should and shouldn't do with the police. We put out our own newspaper, like the Panthers, to inform people in the community.

Our work with CARE and PPP was aimed at bringing these kinds of issues to public attention. It culminated in a protest at the wharves. Immigration tried to load 15 Tongans onto Ocean Monarch. When the crew realised what was happening, they refused to take them. This show of solidarity finally

Roger Fowler and Ama Rauhihi during anti-apartheid protests in New Zealand aimed at stopping the controversial 1981 South African Springbok rugby tour. (Will 'Ilolahia archive).

forced the Government to announce a change in policy the next day.

The Dawn Raids were very hard to combat because they were happening at random and very early in the morning. You must remember it was the 1970s, only 30 years since the War, when people died fighting the same kind of oppression that was happening in our own country. James Baldwin wrote to Angela Davis: 'For if they take you away in the morning they will be coming for us at night.' That rang very true for us. And we thought we had to do something.

It was a time of change and new awareness with Springbok tours – racism was something not just happening in South Africa, but here too.

We used to gather at the Newton PIC. Those who had cars brought them. We would go out and find PIG, follow them around. They were annoyed

and would try and lose us. They would go round the block. I remember one night we approached the Harbour Bridge the wrong way. We knew they would have to come back. So we joined up and followed. They were annoyed but there was nothing they could do. We would just give them basic advice. If you were approached, you would have to provide a driver's licence. But that was about it. Don't have to go to the station unless you are under arrest.

Most of the politicians were from the old school … They (politicians) mostly reflected an older era and had gone through the World War. More traditional in their approach and authority. Couldn't handle the influx of people coming into the country. These immigration policies didn't just affect 'overstayers' but people who had brown faces were also confronted. An intimidating situation.

Working with Citizens' Association for Racial Equality (CARE)

TOM NEWNHAM, MEMBER OF CARE

I suppose like many of our generation we thought that New Zealand was a good place, but we realised there was a lot of hypocrisy. The PIs came to the fore because of the migration began to pick up in the 1970s. On K Road there were more than half were PIs … Particularly with accommodation, Māori and PIs were turned away. I suppose because many of the Islanders who were called overstayers, and came as visitors and so there were raids looking for overstayers so the police found the best way was to come at dawn and that was the Dawn Raids. There were other groups. We all worked together.

The Polynesian Panthers. They were high school kids mainly from Mount Albert Grammar School. With the same aims as us. We had things like photocopiers and access to duplicating machines and these guys were high school kids so we gave them advice. And they would hand out leaflets with that advice at the Grammar School, they would hand them out at K Road … There were plenty of meetings, marches. The students were much more active in those days. They'd have thousands attending. The great thing was we got great results. One tour would be stopped. Then another. Then another. The whole thing was much deeper. This country that had made itself out to be a paragon of values, wasn't. Nineteen eighty-one was the highlight. The South African visits here were organised early. We never had the support of the government. Muldoon made a lot of capital and would provoke us. Protestor became a bad word. He would talk about the violent protestors. The police would patrol the bars. Simply things like hanging up posters they could arrest you for – obstruction.

About that time the police just regarded them as an enemy so it probably came from high up. You look at a rugby match at Eden Park and the majority of players would be PIs. Jonah Lomu would be an overstayer. No problem now …[4]

A Landmark time

JORIS DE BRES, MEMBER OF CITIZENS' ASSOCIATION FOR RACIAL EQUALITY (CARE)

When I came back from overseas, I started an anti-apartheid group. I took over from Tom Newnham. He took me to this hall that was packed with young Tongan workers.

This was a side of New Zealand I hadn't seen before. Then I got to see the conditions they were living in … People were coming here recruited for the labour shortage. It was similar to other countries. They needed workers. Didn't bother with the legalities. They didn't care. People don't migrate for work if there is no work. They were actively encouraged. It was a tidy way to use them and send them home. Very undignified. It all came to a head with the raids.

I can think of one instance, at a Church service at 64 Crummer Road, all of a sudden the doors were knocked in and the place was swarming with police, officials and dogs. They asked for passports. There were 18 that didn't have them, including the priest. They were taken to Mt Eden Prison. The next day, the minister's wife said that we can't take that. I felt great shame at it.

Panthers on the march. Front: Ariu (Lank) Sio. Behind: Nigel Bhana. (John Miller, 1971).

I think initially it was the Immigration Department that called in police to enforce the Immigration Act. If you were unable to provide proof of your passport it was possible to detain you at prison until you could. The reason they did it early was because they knew they could catch people at home. But it was traumatising for the Island community because, regardless of whether you were legal, you didn't know if they were coming for you.

There were some ghastly statements by cabinet ministers that you can identify PIs because they stand out. In the second round of registers, they were going to crack down on people and this started the random checks. The figures I recall were more than 1000 people were stopped and less than 20 were found. Māori were stopped. The ministers said that if you don't look like a New Zealander, then you better carry a passport.

You had a young generation coming through that was more assertive. That had built up because of Treaty claims, which led to Māori land marches. There was a lot of ferment around race relations. Police and government didn't know how to react. One of the reactions was setting up the Police Task Force, which targeted Māori and PIs. They targeted the pubs. The situation was that there was provocation which started problems. There was an upsurge of arrests. There was a climate where people felt oppressed.

The government knew it had a problem with the PI governments. There was concern from them about the raids and the random stops. So the minister, Frank Gill, took a trip to meet with the governments. A group that had been set up had myself and Donna Awatere go over and have meetings. We were able to show them a scrapbook of clippings that they were able to confront him with. He encountered a lot of hostility. It was known in the islands but the minister had decided not to have New Zealand journalists on his plane. So it was unreported and unknown. There was a snubbing of Frank Gill by the people. There were lots of signals. That was a time when you could go away and not have it reported. He came back and said it all went really well. It was a shocking state of affairs.

When I got involved in these issues, nowhere in our schools was there taught anything about the Pacific. I had to look up where Tonga was. No-one had an awareness of the Pacific. There was more awareness of apartheid in South Africa.

It's like any time. The ordinary police were acting under orders. There were people in the police who did not feel at all comfortable about the whole process. But I think the police have come a long way. This was the old New Zealand, which blew apart in the 1970s with Māori language, etc. Things like the Springbok Tour that changed us. You can't judge them by today's standards and have to see them for when they were. But people were uncomfortable. It was a landmark time.

CARE was a multiracial organisation that arose out of the early days of the race movement. We actually ended up with a whole awareness campaign and close scrutiny of things … I, like many New Zealanders, knew little and was learning quickly. There was a high level of media interest. I also got involved with bailing people out after being arrested by the Task Force. I always remember the instance of daylight savings when I arrive at 8 and they put the clock back. The police asked an Islander what his name was and he said 'Whakaofo', and they arrested him for offensive language.[5]

Ngā Tamatoa
HONE HARAWIRA

I think we were just starting to come out of a time when all brownies were just brownies and into a time when people were wanting to be clearer about who they were, where they were from, that kind of thing. I was young already when the Panthers and Ngā Tamatoa got started, I was still at school, I never really got into it until about 1973. I remember seeing Will 'Ilolahia speak at some hui in Otara when he gave his now-famous line about 'the only difference between you Māori and the rest of us Pacific Islanders was that you came on a waka and we came on a jet …'

And up until then, I myself had never really seen us as being particularly different … everybody was … everybody [was] brown anyway … was pretty much the same. The Polynesian Panthers was different because they were trying to establish a broader thing … Ngā Tamatoa at the time and they were very very focused on the status of Māori as tangata whenua and re-establishing that mana, re-establishing the importance of the reo, and our rights as an indigenous people in our own land … I was very focused on that sort of thing and interacted with the Panthers on various activities that we were involved and directly with members of the Panthers in specific protest activity that wasn't either Panther or Tamatoa it was pretty much just straight Polynesian activity …

I'm ashamed to say that I never really realised how many Pacific Islanders I was raised with … until I started running into them over the last few months, you know, just touring round Auckland particularly as part of the Māori Party thing and then just running into men and women I'd gone to school with … there was a whole heap of them from Samoa, Tonga, Niue, Tokelau … but again … we were brought up … I never thought of myself as being Māori and them being something else … we were brought up to be who we were … we were just all brownies … naturally brownies …

WAS THERE MUCH SUPPORT FOR P.I.S WITH DAWN RAIDS ETC. FROM MĀORI?

… I think for a lot of Māori they were sort of standing back because they didn't want to be next … if you know what I mean … so I don't think outside of the Ngā Tamatoa environment there was a lot of empathy or as much empathy as there could have been for what was happening … it was bloody shocking really what was happening … but Māori generally didn't play that much of a role in fighting it … I know Ngā Tamatoa did … I know that members of the New Zealand Māori Council raised issues about it … I know that the people that I hung out with tendered to want to make an issue of it … but my feel of the general Māori community was that it really wasn't an issue …

1970S PROTEST MOVEMENT

It was a new time then … we were the young ones and the baby boomers … internationally people were opposing the Vietnam War … there was the rise of the Black Panthers … the American Indian movement … that sort of thing was staring to rise right across the Western World so when it finally came to pass here we were part of that time … and so our time was completely different to what it is now … there was not respect for any of the Pacific cultures … there was no respect for Māori culture … no recognition of Māori language … back then Māori were still seen to be the ones working on the road works and playing guitars at the pub … that was about it really … there wasn't a heck of a lot of respect for the role that we played as tangata whenua or our connection to people from the Pacific – it was very much not part of the normal world … so we grew up in a time when we came into adulthood at a time when those things were just starting to be expressed … so were a part of that …

HE TAUA

… the Panthers had their headquarters down opposite the Gluepot … Hilda and I we stayed here … down on Collingwood Street … and in fact it was from there that we launched He Taua … which was the raid on the Auckland University students who had been up until that time bastardising the haka as well as making fun of Pacific Island culture – it wasn't just about the haka – and when we went up … the people I picked to go … on that raid … were pretty much half-Māori half-Pacific Islander … from Otara and from Ponsonby here … none of us were University students because I had already heard from my wife that the students didn't really want to do anything that caused trouble … so I picked people who I knew I could count on in a situation like that.. I didn't go round looking to get particularly Māori or particularly Pacific Islander, just the people I knew I could count on, and they were as much Pacific Islanders as they were Māori … that was the world we walked in at the time … and that was the world I was proud to be part of …

… Those were good times … we were young then … we were hot-blooded … we were bulletproof … yeah, we weren't actually … but we all certainly thought we were … we had the fire to change the world and we didn't care who agreed with us or who disagreed with us … we were going to change the world … and I'm as proud of my relationships with all of those people [Panthers] now as I was then … even the fact that some of those people went on to be priests and policemen – it doesn't change anything … I look back on the things that we went through during those times and they were good times …[6]

1981 Springbok protest: Patu Squad

INTERVIEW WITH WILL AND HONE

TELL US ABOUT THE SIGNIFICANCE OF THIS SITE IN 1981 …

Will: We were members of the Patu Squad in '81 and we were set the task to take a group of people into the park and we had prearranged with a gang – which I won't name – but they were in there in the house next door to the park and probably it was the only time that a lot of the street gangs got together … plus the political groups of Māori and Pacific Islanders …

Hone: When I got there we needed some organisation and I looked around and thought shit who's going to organise a motley crew like this? … I spotted this fella across and the crowd and … so Will and I worked out how we were going to organise it because as Will was saying we had different groups, not a lot of whom got along well with one another …

HOW DID YOU MANAGE HAVING BOTH MĀORI AND PACIFIC TOGETHER?

Will: I think by that time, Patu Squad had got a bit of a reputation as being a so-called brown people's squad against the Springbok Tour and so a lot of Māori and Pacific Islands people came together for that day and a lot of them came for the Patu Squad, but like Hone said we had arranged for a group and we were trying to disguise it in such a way that we could … hid[e] the Squad and so with Hone's help we were able to try and do a diversion group to go up and for us to come down here … because this was like the last one and we thought we would all do a big battle … and consequently I think it was raised in our court case that out of 36 of the red squad, 24 were permanently injured …

Hone: In fact, as Will was saying, the reputation of the Patu Squad had grown over the time so that by the time we got to Fowlds Park or some park down the road here … Gribblehirst or something … a lot of Polynesian community, brothers anyway, just came looking for the Patu Squad and as soon as they saw the signs they just sort of fit in with the lines there … it was a good day … it was a very good day in terms of an expression of how we were feeling in this country and what was happening in South Africa … but I'd say a lot for what was happening in this country …

WHAT HAPPENED AT THE TOP OF ONSLOW?

Will: … What we found there was a police car that was actually on the road and so we overturned it and basically informed the people there that we knew where they were … that was one of the major problems we had in organising this because there were undercover police in the squad and so it was very difficult and very secretive and that was why Hone and I were sort of back and forth, back and forth without anyone knowing …

WHAT DO YOU THINK THE SIGNIFICANCE OF THIS WAS FOR PACIFIC ISLANDERS AT THE TIME?

Will: I think it was probably the first time too that a lot of Pacific Islanders – outside of the groups like Ngā Tamatoa or the Panthers – were involved in a street protest and that was the thing that I think was major for the Pacific Island community, it was the first time that they were involved in something confrontative like this and I think also it united a lot of us Māori and Pacific Islanders cause there was a lot of work that came out of this and although it was the last event for the Panthers in some ways it set up some steadfast relationships between us …

HOW DID IT CHANGE YOUR LIVES?

Hone: … I don't think that this event changed either Will or myself … we were already on this sort of line anyway this was just taking it to another level in terms of fighting the racism as we saw it here and an opportunity to link that fight with the fight internationally …

Will: For me … after my trial in '83 I didn't feel like a Kiwi anymore because I thought that we did something for Aotearoa so I left for Tonga to go and find out my roots and that was the effect that it had on me … but politically, as Hone said, it actually didn't change us at all … just for me personally, I didn't feel like a Kiwi at all after this …

OTHER COMMENTS

Hone: I still look on those with good feelings for those I marched with and fought with – fought alongside – and I don't feel any shame whatsoever for standing up for what we believed in and the way we stood up in those days and I'm proud to have been a member of the Patu squad with this guy and everyone else who was here on that day …[7]

ENDNOTES

[1] Poata-Smith, E. T. H. cited in Anae, M. (1998) *Fofoaivaoese: Identity Journeys of New Zealand-born Samoans.* Unpublished PhD dissertation, Anthropology, University of Auckland, p.237.

[2] Anae, M. (1998) *Fofoaivaoese: Identity Journeys of New Zealand-born Samoans.* Unpublished PhD dissertation, Anthropology, University of Auckland, p.238.

[3] *Te Manu Korihi programme.* 6 June 2014, Radio New Zealand National.

[4] *Dawn Raids.* 5 June 2005, TV One. Auckland: Isola Productions.

[5] *Dawn Raids.* 5 June 2005, TV One. Auckland: Isola Productions.

[6] Excerpt from *Panui Pasifika: Protest.* 25 January 2006, Māori Television.

[7] Excerpt from *Panui Pasifika: Protest.* 25 January 2006, Māori Television.

ALL POWER TO
THE
STOP ALL U.S. IMPERIALIST PIGS
GREATER LOVE HATH NO MAN
POLYNESIAN.
PANTHER
CHEMIST

FROM POLYNESIAN PANTHER MOVEMENT TO POLYNESIAN PANTHER PARTY

'Power to the People'

The Polynesian Panther Movement (PPM) grew ever more politicised, which rapidly led to changes in its activities, tactics and outlook. In November 1972, a little more than a year after its formation, these changes were reflected in a major transformation in its structure, when the movement became a political party, the Polynesian Panther Party (PPP). Official positions included: coordinator; chairman, secretary, minister of defence, minister of information, minister of culture, minister of supply, chief of Panther Youth, captain, agents and investigators.

Its status as a bona fide group was recognised in a number of ways. Notably, the PPP was awarded the governor general's Youth Award in September 1972. The appointment of Ama Rauhihi (minister of culture) as the PPP's full-time community worker signalled the Panthers' commitment to working at the grass-roots level. It also meant the PPP needed more financial resources to pay Ama's wages (to be $2,000 a year from 1973). An annual grant of $1,000 from the National Council of Churches provided some of this monetary support.

In addition, the PPP developed an official platform and promoted it vigorously. This document was crucial as it outlined the PPP's goals and objectives.

A legal aid booklet was published and widely circulated among Pacific communities. This legal aid booklet was the culmination of fierce determination by the Panthers and a lot of support from Palagi supporters – people like David Lange, then a budding lawyer, another young lawyer, Robert Ludbrooke, who went on to set up the Grey Lynn Neighbourhood Law Office, Roger Fowler, Coordinator of the People's Union, who actually helped print the legal aid booklet, Tom Newnham and Joris de Bres, members of CARE (Citizens Association for Racial Equality). These 'white on white' activist organisations all worked together with the Panthers with 'Equality for all' as their main catch-cry. The community spirit was strong amongst the Panthers and all these groups and together with Ngā Tamatoa let the establishment know that all was not well, that there definitely were injustices in New Zealand society and that so called 'racial harmony' in New Zealand was a farce.

New Zealand Herald February 1977

Panthers Having to Leave Their Lair

Things came to a head when the police started harassing Panther members and supporters culminating in their Headquarters in Ponsonby being vandalised by the Police and they were forced to move to Redmond St.

All in all, the crucible years for the Panthers provided a platform for change in Palagi attitudes towards Pacific peoples. They started realising that not all Pacific Islanders were rapists, thugs or just 'coconuts'. There was a new generation of educated, savvy and committed Pacific Islanders who were proud of their heritage as Pacific Islanders in New Zealand, and who were not taking any more 'bullshit' from the establishment.

The last official act of the Panthers before going 'under cover' was taking part in the Springbok Protests in 1981. They stood side by side, alongside other New Zealanders who would not tolerate the Apartheid regime embodied in the acceptance of the Springbok Rugby team coming to New Zealand.

Remembering the PPP experience

FUIMAONO NORMAN TUIASAU

Talofa lava, malo lelei, and warm Pacific greetings. I must first confess that these thoughts are based on a massive jumble of recollections, and on a flawed and self-serving memory. It should not be read as a true and accurate record of what may have happened, but simply to record, before it is too late, some of my unrepressed, and as I write this some repressed, reminiscences of that amazing time in my life, many years ago. Therefore these stories should be approached with a great deal of caution because they are recalled with a good deal of hindsight and fondness, so are not unbiased. However, as we are told now by even the most well-meaning cynic, 'Even impressions can count for a reality.'

I think that the context of these experiences is just as important as the experiences themselves. It was at a time of great economic, social and political change throughout the Western world. In the late 1960s and early 1970s, liberal and radical politics spread across Europe and the Americas. Major events around the world threw up issues, heroes and paradoxes. The Vietnam War was a catalyst for many. New heroes emerged for us like Ho Chi Minh and General Van Nguyen Giap. We all identified with Muhammad Ali, for example, when he refused to be drafted in the Vietnam War; especially with his reasoning, 'No Vietcong called me a nigger.'

South Africa's apartheid regime continued to shock and bewilder us, regardless of the farcical attempts of the South African regime and the West to negotiate with their chosen black leaders. As countries across the African continent decolonised, Patrick Lumumba of Zaire and Julius Nyerere of Tanzania became our mentors.

Other events that fuelled our sense of purpose were the United Kingdom Campaign for Nuclear Disarmament; the Brixton riots and killing of Palagi New Zealander Blair Peach (by United Kingdom police); and the assassination of Chile's first democratically elected leader, Allende, as probably ordered by General Pinochet.

Writers of the time who helped to radicalise me and many others included Noam Chomsky, with his views on the imperialistic and destructive streak of Western culture; Samir Amin and Andre Frank, on colonialism and unequal development; Ivan Illich; James Baldwin; Franz Fanon; Fidel Castro and Che Guevara; Romero Chavez; Karl Marx (especially his discussion in *Das Kapital* of the colonisation of New Zealand); and Kath Walker of Australia. My views of colonialism and the American Indian experience were also influenced by Dee Dee Williams' *Bury My Heart at Wounded Knee*.

Musical anthems also expressed our purpose. Jimi Hendrix's 'Machine Gun', the Four Tops' 'Papa was a Rolling Stone', Isaac Hay's 'Shaft', Stevie Wonder's 'Living in the City', Miles Davis' 'Bitches Brew' and 'Sketches of Spain' and many others told of change, courage and uncertainty. Bob Dylan was always niggling away at us in the background. It was a swelter of energy, questioning, and finding identity.

Yet through all this, I can still remember listening to the soul song, 'What the World Needs Now is Love Sweet Love' and Marvin Gaye singing, 'What's Going On' while going to Church at the Newton and then the Onehunga PIC, and being involved with the PPP.

It was interesting, looking back now, to see our sense of identity with Black political protest leaders was never the same for all of us. I do not think we could all relate to the Black Panthers in the USA.

But we could relate to the United States Black Power movement and the parallels with slavery and migrant labour issues, and the struggle against institutional racism. I think we all had our individual United States heroes from that time: Huey Newton, the president of the Black Panthers; or Elridge Cleaver, who wrote *Seize the Time*, a Soledad brother like George Jackson, or Malcolm X or Dr Martin Luther King Jr. Some of us also identified with Black women writers who used the pen to enlighten and change attitudes; women like Alice Walker and Toni Morrison. Then there was Angela

These newspaper headlines concern Ama Rauhihi (on the right), a Panther and trained social worker who became a community worker for the Polynesian Panther Party, partly funded by the $1000 donated by the National Council of Churches in 1973. (*City and West End News*, November 1972 and *New Zealand Herald*, April 1973).
'Silent migrants' documented a request by sociologist Dr Cluny Macpherson to 'listen carefully to groups like the Polynesian Panthers, which the public had labelled as "misfits"...' as part of the University of Auckland Winter Lectures on social policy and its implications for the equality of Polynesian immigrants.
(*New Zealand Herald*, 12 July 1973).

Davis, who wrote, *When the Morning Comes*, a highly charged polemic. Branded by the FBI one of the ten most dangerous people in the USA, she was tried for murder and kidnapping but was found not guilty after being in jail for a year! It endeared her to us even more.

The Pacific was also changing. Tonga's monarchy was suppressing the free press and democracy; it's still going on! Dr Futa Helu touched us all with his sage-like qualities of profound wisdom mixed with a sense of humour. Fiji, Tonga, Papua New Guinea and Tuvalu became independent in the 1970s. The opposition to French atmospheric nuclear testing on Mururoa, Tahiti was also a cause we all strongly identified with …

In Auckland, challenging society and the community attitudes and beliefs in regard to Pacific people is what I remember about my time with the PPP. There was always something 'going on' with the PPP.

We were being radicalised from all quarters and extremities. But part of our radicalisation came about as Pacific youth and leaders, trying to make sense of Pacific Island cultural issues and practices in the new Pacific urban environment. This was a monumental task. It was always a challenge to relate the idyllic, coral-atoll lifestyles, traditions and beliefs of our parents to our new urban Western experiences. Some of our parents supported us when we could explain our shared immigrant experiences of hardship as being scapegoated and being at the bottom of the social ladder. However, other Pacific parents thought we were culturally and socially ignorant and would question us, often at home. Like the children of other immigrant communities settling and adjusting to their new world, we were always walking a fine line between supporting our Pacific parents, Pacific languages and cultural practices, and challenging our

communities through our own experiences; seeing and bringing new ways of thinking and doing things to our communities. I remember when we were challenged by the Pacific Churches about poverty; we were labelled as Fia Palagi communists.

Christchurch Star   June 1973

Polynesian Panthers: Words, not guns

There were activities, programmes and protests. One thing that stood out was the police harassment of Pacific Islanders. Among our more overtly political acts were to form PIG patrols in response to police harassment of Pacific Islanders; support for community safety by lobbying for traffic lights on the corner of Ponsonby Rd and Franklin Rd; protest against the Vietnam War, with many other groups and individuals; public talks about issues facing PI youth and the Palagi education system; homework centres for Ponsonby youth. Supporting Māori activists in their struggle for the recognition of te reo Māori and tikanga Māori was important for all of us in Auckland, at Waitangi and around New Zealand. We also celebrated with Māori the opening of marae, including the marae at Mangakino. To now read the Waitangi Tribunal Report on te reo and Māori land claims (most of them vindicated) makes me, and no doubt many others in the PPP, feel proud to have been

Polynesian Panthers as part of the anti-apartheid protests in New Zealand aimed at stopping the controversial 1981 South African Springbok rugby tour. Will 'Ilolahia pictured far right.
(Will 'Ilolahia archive).

a very small part of our Māori cousins' struggles for this recognition. Will 'Ilolahia opened our eyes to the issues facing tangata whenua. Syd and Hana Jackson, and Titiwhai Harawira, also taught us so much. They were always supportive of our activities. They always invited us to their activities and functions which we were glad to support.

Australia's Communist Weekly   July 1972

N.Z. Black Panther Here

'N.Z. Black Panther Here' refers to Will 'Ilolahia's visit to Canberra in support of the Aboriginal Embassy in 1972. Will was arrested. (*Tribune: Australia's Communist Weekly*, 4–10 July 1972, p.1).

Among the many moments and events I remember, these are some of the defining ones for me:

- Tom Hodges got into strife because he wanted to blame some lone Palagi cop on Ponsonby Rd for institutional racism. We had to get out of that situation before he got arrested.
- The Team Policing Unit arrived at the Kiwi Tavern, where some of us were under-age drinking. We pretended to be FOBs and that we couldn't understand anything the police were asking us! Luckily a fight broke out across the bar and we all disappeared.
- We were protesting at Waitangi when Queen Elizabeth II walked through a guard of honour made up of Scouts dressed up like the Brown Shirt fascists of Italy. It got on the front cover of the *New Zealand Herald*.
- I met Futa Helu of the Atenisi Institute, Nukualofa, Tonga. We lost a debating competition to the Paremoremo Prisoners Debating Club (New Zealand champs at the time). We were escorted out of Parliament in Wellington from the Select Committee hearing on changes to the Child Youth and Families Act, after Tom Hodges told the Chair of the Committee to shut up because he was treating our group like we were children. When we met Vietnamese diplomats who were ex soldiers in Auckland, and Will 'Ilolahia spoke to them in French.
- We built good relationships and friendships with our Palagi colleagues.
- Wayne Toleafoa quoted Cat Stevens: 'It's hard but it's harder to ignore it.'
- I heard Angela Davies speak in Berlin, East Germany at a Youth Conference.
- In Red Square, Moscow, I saw Lenin's grave.
- I heard Māori radicals at Waitangi talk about the Treaty.
- I went to Jerusalem, Wanganui, with another Panther after J K Baxter's death, and then learned about the struggles of Taranaki Māori with the government. Being there under the mountain made the legacy and history so vivid and just unbelievable.
- When Will, Tigi and I and a couple of other PPP members 'dawn raided' the minister of immigration …

We had a manifesto, which I couldn't quite relate to; we had portfolio positions which were above me. The issues we were dealing with were so varied, complex and exciting. Yet with the personnel we had (many of us were just secondary school students), what we achieved was quite remarkable.

Raising awareness seems to be a big thing for us. It was to try and get the general public to look at racism, and to see the Pacific community as a treasure trove with many assets, and not a population with crime or health problems. It almost seems that we have come full circle: 'What has gone around has indeed come around.'

It was a swelter of energy, questioning and trying to find identity.

Ia fa'amanuia lava le taumafai o tatou uma. Tofa soifua.

Special Assignment
MELANI ANAE

After my first year at Varsity … because I had passed all my papers … my father and oldest brother, who worked for Air New Zealand, 'shouted' me a trip to the United States to visit my auntie and uncle in Compton, Los Angeles. I was to stay for two months over the summer. When the Polynesian Panthers heard about this, they saw it as an opportunity to make contact with the Black Panthers, in the States! I remember thinking …Me??? Contact them???? Me … a mere Samoan girl from Auckland, New Zealand??? I felt a nervous twinge and pushed the thought aside. I enjoyed staying with my aunty heaps, even though they were Mormon, meaning we never got to go out that much. They took me through the black township of Watts though, and I remember my cousin saying, 'No-one ever stops their car when driving through Watts, you don't stop you just

keep driving through … it's too dangerous' … This made me even more nervous and I cowered in anticipation of the 'job' I had been sent there to do. My dad and brother probably would have throttled me if they knew!!! I waited until my very last day in the States, found their number in the phone-book (Who else could I ask?), then gathered up enough courage to make the dreaded phone-call: … 'Black Panther Headquarters … Hello … Hello …??' I responded, feeling six inches tall, 'Hi! My name is … I'm from … I'd just like to tell you how our group supports you and that you have a Polynesian chapter in Auckland New Zealand.' 'Who??? From where???' … I had been talking to a Black Panther's sister I think it was … She was very gracious and I felt that a huge load had been lifted from my shoulders. When I got back to New Zealand, a bunch of reading material/ pamphlets arrived from the States. I had done my job, the leaders were pleased with my effort. I could relax.[1]

Profiling Victor Tamati

AS REPORTED BY THE *NEW ZEALAND HERALD*, 2001

Last weekend former Panthers and friends, extended families and former foes talked among themselves again. At their reunion other issues were discussed … and some old animosities resolved. One who left the Panthers in disgust, in part over disagreement with 'Ilolahia, was there. Former South Auckland PPP chairman, Tamati came up from the South Island, where he has long been a youth worker, because what he believed back there hasn't changed. 'I've always perpetrated that message and the image we gave of the panther was it was a docile animal. It lives, it feeds and sits in trees and enjoys life. But corner a panther and you've got a whole different beast – it comes out on the offensive. I've always operated that same psychological and mental attitude in everything I do. I'll work with your systems, I'll work with you. But don't put me or my people down – because I'll come out fighting.'

New Zealand Herald   June 1976

Panthers Call Meeting

The PPP was divided into two chapters, one in Ponsonby, the other in South Auckland headed by Aorere College student Victor Tamati who, because he was a schoolboy, found it hard to be taken seriously by the police J-team with whom he wanted to work on youth projects. And even more so by local gangs. So where the city chapter deliberately targeted gangs for members, Tamati had to adopt a different approach.

'I couldn't change those older guys, they were lock and load on where they were. My thinking was to encourage the younger ones to look at the way they were living. I wanted to change the future, not the present, and that's where Will and I differed. He wanted me to bring in the fighters.'

But South Auckland gangs thought the PPP was just another street gang from central Auckland out to take their patch. Tamati says he was fighting so often he felt he was moving into that lifestyle rather than away from it.

'So no, we didn't get our point across. South Auckland was fast growing to be a Once Were Warriors place. Everyone around me was either joining the Black Power or the Mongrel Mob and I was trying to say, 'Let's go political.'[2]

Billy Bates

I joined the Panthers because at the time we were constantly getting hassled by police and being stopped for petty little reasons so the Panthers opened the opportunity where as we could sort what really was going on at the time. At the time I was involved in setting up the legal aid book and organising people who had to go to court or needed lawyers and things like that like free legal aid …

I was basically on my own to a great extent … but being in the Panthers gave me a better perspective on what really goes on in the world in regards to relationships between whether it be Pākehā and Māori, or Polynesians and Māori, or the whole mix … And how the government works as well.

At the time there were Māori in the Polynesian Panthers as well so we got on really well together. Ngā Tamatoa were very sympathetic to the Pacific Island cause, but in some aspects I think they were more political … that's just my own opinion … I think at the time groups such as Ngā Tamatoa … were busy with their own agendas, as we were busy with ours, and I think we were both sort of sympathetic to each other …

As far as the [1975] Land March was concerned, I started from Te Unga Waka in Newmarket and walked to Wellington. I actually carried the Pou Whenua from Otaki Marae halfway through Wellington which was the last stretch …

I think I still have the fire and passion in me now … what we were trying to achieve in those days was just to make life better for people … because people were constantly being hassled by police … you had the Dawn Raids … all those sort of things … You had bad landlords … throwing people out on the streets for no reason … So we were kept busy.

For the Pacific Island people you go back to the Dawn Raids … The Panthers were the ones who instigated the stopping of that sort of carry on … and I think we made people more aware of what they are entitled to, how to go about getting things done for their family or anything legal … whereas before they didn't have a clue.[3]

Perspective from a Dunedin PPP member

MERE MEANATA MONTGOMERIE

My grounding in [the] PPP [Polynesian Panther Party] was in Auckland at the end of 1971, in my seventh form year. One of the motivating reasons for getting into PPP was … an incident of racism by a landlord. At the time we had Fijian-Indian friends staying at home, and I (with my good English) rang around trying to find accommodation. When I mentioned their name, Singh, or my own surname M E A N A T A the response changed to 'Oh, I have someone already looking at it', or something more derogatory.

In 1972, I went to Tonga on Volunteer Service Abroad – imagine that: sending a Tongan Māori to Tonga. Anyway, one of the tasks I had from the PPP (namely Cuzzy Will) was to meet with the king. I had a letter from the PPP to advise him about the plight of the Tongan families in New Zealand. The nearest I got was to the Queen Mataaho; politics at that level wasn't her forte.

8 o'clock   February 1977

Why Panther Boys Dug In

I returned at the end of 1972 and resumed contact with the PPP but was sent to Dunedin (that's another story) to Otago University to study law … In June 1973, Will 'Ilolahia and Billy Bates visited Dunedin. They made the headlines in their black garb and beret (couldn't fit a beret on my afro). They were sponsored by the university and some Church organisations. They had a round of radio interviews, public meetings and a capacity audience at the Student Union of Otago.

The Dunedin PPP began shortly after this visit … my flatmate, the late Sandy Edwards, roped in Esther Taylor, Mike Stevens, Donna Waipouri and several other supporters. Our activities included the establishment of a homework centre in the basement of Burns Hall, prison visits to the Dunedin Women's Prison and some legal aid via a good supportive lawyer.

The PPP received support from the Student Christian Movement based at Otago University, HART,

Otago University Māori Club, Community Volunteers and Ngā Tamatoa.

The PPP ceased to function in Dunedin in 1975. At that time I got married and moved out of Dunedin city, and I didn't have a car or a licence to allow me to continue with PPP activities.

ENDNOTES

[1] Excerpt, with minor editing, from Anae, M. (2003) 'O a'u/I: My Identity Journey'. In Fairbairn Dunlop, P. and Makisi, G. (Eds) *Making Our Place: Growing up PI in New Zealand.* Palmerston North: Dunmore Press.

[2] *New Zealand Weekend Herald*, 23 June 2001, E4.

[3] Excerpt from *Panui Pasifika: Protest.* 25 January 2006, Māori Television.

PART SIX

'ONCE A PANTHER, ALWAYS A PANTHER'

Even when their formal involvement with the Panthers ended, many members have remained Panthers in terms of their firm commitment to combating all forms of racism, through a variety of strategies – anywhere that they work, play, do business or make music. They also continue to share an intense drive to mentor and support Pacific youth in realising their full potential by drawing on their Pacific cultures and heritages, and developing their professional skills as New Zealanders.

and families – are what has provided them with the impetus to seek to change the status quo. This progression from personal experience to professional action is a product of the socio-political and historical context of Pacific peoples growing up in New Zealand in the 1960s and 1970s. Some Panthers recall how as young Pacific Island school leavers they were actively recruited into government departments to cope with the expanding Pacific population, especially in the urban areas of Auckland and Wellington.

New Zealand Truth   June 2001

Never Thugs! Polynesian Panthers reunite to keep the faith

In combination, the occupations and activities of all Panther members who tell their stories in this book are concerned with elevating Pacific people in the educational, philosophical, secular and spiritual spheres, thus removing their status in New Zealand society as second-rate citizens. It is no accident that so many Panthers are in professions and occupations in which they can initiate social change for Pacific peoples from within the system or act as guardians of Pacific peoples when they brush with the law or misunderstand the bureaucratic structure. Panthers state definitively that their dealings with the system – their personal experiences and their observations of what was happening to their peers

Some studied to become teachers, social workers, chefs, musicians, youth advocates; others to become ministers and missionaries. Those who were able to support and associate with tangata whenua became politically savvy and turned these skills towards helping their own Pacific communities. It became an assertion of their own Pacific ethnic identity. Some members went to university, where they became not only intellectually stimulated but also involved in political activities on campus. For many, the university experience was an opportunity to 'reclaim' their identity and to juxtapose their New Zealand-born or secured Pacific knowledges and belief systems against Palagi intellectual systems and movements. It contributed significantly to their critical analysis of what was happening to, or happening for, Pacific peoples living in New Zealand so that they could understand and put into perspective issues of racism, inequality, feminism, the gay movement, power and knowledge. More importantly, university education helped to explain Panther members' experience and understandings of the subordinate position of Pacific peoples in New Zealand society. Some reacted positively to other movements such as feminism, others negatively, but the shared outcome was a deeper insight into what they knew of unequal power relations.

The 30th anniversary reunion held in June 2001 was a chance for a catchup for all the Panthers who were able to attend. Members who had passed on were remembered, and the new generation of the children of Panthers who were continuing the Panther tradition of knowing where you come from in going forward, was acknowledged – Che Fu and Victor Tamati's girls and others. Talk also revolved around the need to document Panther experiences and the idea of a book, maybe even a movie, was born. We also noticed how worn and tired and 'grey-haired' most of the Panthers had become. But nothing could take their Panther experiences from them. The crucible years of the Panthers were when it all happened. They put Ponsonby on the map, the PI in Pacific Islanders and started the revolution for recognition of the browning of New Zealand soon to come. They did all this as 17–19 year olds and were recognised not only by our Pacific communities but also by the Government of New Zealand and the Black Panthers in the United States for their work.

Post-Polynesian Panthers

WILL 'ILOLAHIA

Thirty-four years after I took part in setting up the PPP (Polynesian Panther Party) in New Zealand, I'm still affected by its effective programmes and beliefs. I describe my present occupation as a social entrepreneur, yet even Auckland's deputy mayor, Rev. Bruce Hucker, has translated this to be the PC word for a shit-stirrer. Revolution means change … that is what I've been doing although I myself, I admit, haven't changed.

April 20 I couldn't attend the 35th anniversary of the United States Black Panther Party on advice from the Ministry of Foreign Affairs personnel not to travel to America, as there was a high chance I'd spend my entire US trip at the airport security lock up. This was not my idea of meeting the United States Panthers in person for the first time.

In 1984, on returning to Tonga after a two-year trial for my participation in the infamous anti-Springbok Patu Squad, I was questioned by the local police: 'Why are you still in Tonga after six months?' The basis of their concern was that, according to them, I was listed on a SIS/CIA top ten table of known Pacific 'activists'. I laughed it off especially when they were led to believe I was in Tonga to kill the king.

Gee, all I did was assist Ngati Whatua win back Bastion Point, provide Nelson Mandela (as he said himself) 'inspiration' to become president and end apartheid, and establish homework centres, tenants' protection and food co-operatives, which are now part of mainstream government policies.

Actually I was in Tonga to learn about my roots after years of fighting for Māori land rights and te reo, being a Panther, the Springbok Tour to name a few. In 1984, I was glad we had a monarchy. These days I am concerned that the Westernised education provided to the royal children is corrupting a disciplined society that is centuries old.

During that visit, the late Ve'ehala (Queen Salote's cultural adviser/librarian) not only taught me about my own lineage, but also about our Tongan 2000 BC Tui Tonga empire. That made me even more proud of what I had stood for during my PPP days.

Being a Tongan and taking my Bastion Point conviction to the Privy Council of the United Kingdom and getting off by quoting the Magna Carta enhanced our PPP belief of all being Polynesian. We used to jokingly explain, 'The only difference between a Māori and Pacific Islander is the Māori came to Aotearoa by waka, we PIs decided to require the Palagi to give us a jet … far easier …'

Throughout my post-Panther days, the PPP doctrines I had learnt formed my foundation as a social entrepreneur.

Pioneering anti-nuclear music as manager of Herbs, Detach Youth work with street gangs, setting up rugby league in the Pacific, assisting many born-again Māori and other Polynesians realise their whakapapa/roots, giving production assistance for Bob Geldolf's Sport Aid concert from Tonga, setting up senior citizen activities in One Tree Hill as a council officer, being a Commonwealth fellowship recipient … for these and many other activities I adapted PPP doctrines.

ONCE ATTACKED, THE PANTHER …

During my 'rugby league days', besides staging the first games and setting up league in the Kingdom, I was honoured to manage the only Tongan sports team to make a world cup final – the 1992 students' rugby league team.

After coming through a hard draw to beat England and Ireland, we were set to face Australia in the semis, following the usual convention of first-ranked team playing the fourth-ranked. Thank God for a printing error. It meant a semi against New Zealand (ranked second) – on the way we had to pay them $1,500 to release two of our players. My world cup final was in the board room. In the debate over the draw, I had support from the other PI nations – PNG, Samoa and Fiji. Pointing out that the programme draw had been printed out well before tournament started, I asked why now – when an Island team makes it – a call for change? I informed them that the Island nations would pull out from future participation. Their meetings with other PIs confirmed that the old 'divide and rule' or 'we are just islanders' syndrome didn't wash with this coconut … we won to play New Zealand.

Prior to the semi I stuck up a banner in the changing room announcing New Zealand had cost us $1,500. Our team of mainly Senior B players beat New Zealand 24–11 and made the finals. The Ozzie team was, as usual, a different class, but we made it into the finals.

Also, managing Herbs – the whole MARK XV versions (membership changes were MARK …) – relied heavily on my PPP chairman experiences of dealing with over 500 members, supporters and family in 13 chapters throughout Aotearoa.

UNEMPLOYABLE

An integral part of being a pioneer is to instigate or set up events. Achieving social change is rewarding especially when the outcome is positive for a significant part of society. I learnt through being in a Panther, pioneering on many extreme front lines.

But, like the dialectic of materialism outlined in some of our sociology studies in the 1960s and 1970s, being straight and truthful also brought its downfalls, especially in some of the systems one has to survive in …

2004: How many more job interviews, then rejections can I take? (At the time of this story, 2004, I've been shortlisted for several government positions, managerial roles, but pipped at the post every time …) I start to wonder whether I should provide Grey Power with a military wing – at least the MW got things done – just to get us over 50-year-olds some respect. Man we've got page loads of well-earned experience … I've got a part-time job at a PI radio station because that's all my worth. Sometimes I wonder if it was worth it. Fighting to create opportunities like NIU FM and then not being recognised for it … Looks like people are still being ripped off, not only by the system but by our own! Even now in the 21st century. I wonder?

Panthers celebrating 30-year anniversary of the formation of the Polynesian Panther Party.
From left to right: Ta Iuli, Aloma Ahmu Wehi, Paddy Minola, Melani Anae, Victor Tamati, Lusi Atiga, Will 'Ilolahia. (Will 'Ilolahia archive).

ENDING ... OR IS IT ANOTHER BEGINNING?

As I write this, aged 53 now, after dying twice (GBS '96 Auckland hospital), wheelchaired for over one year, teenage/adult siblings bringing tears to my eyes, I hear Katie Melua sing, 'the closest thing to craziness is living with me ...'

Being a Panther, now social entrepreneur, has been a crazy existence not only for myself, but for the people around me. But it's been a positive effect. Surveying all the things I've achieved in life, I'm glad I was part of the global Panther Party experience, being arrested for standing up on behalf of Māori land rights (Bastion Point), Aboriginal Embassy (Canberra, Australia, 1972), against racists in Avondale (jailed six months, 1974), providing legal aid in PIG patrols, (Tenants Aid Brigade) protection protests, and anti-war 'no Vietcong called me a coconut' protests. I was also part of the anti-Springbok Patu Squad on trial for two years until Bishop Desmond Tutu of Soweto convinced the jury that I and 12 others were freedom fighters. Verdict: not guilty.

Even after my PPP term, my Panther beliefs carried over into managing Herbs. I took on Randy Crawford's 'Music speaks louder than words' as a belief and toured with Herbs and others such as The Jets and UB40, utilising music to create social change in Australasia. Although it wasn't a total revolution, I must admit there have been some improvements in areas I have had a chance to be present in. During 2005 and 2006 I co-produced a 13-part television series, *Panui Pasifika*, for Māori Television, a pioneering show bringing Māori and Pacific together – so I'm still at it!

Now I can leave it to our offspring Che Fu, Scribe, All Black Ben Atiga and many others to carry on the work in their own way ...

Dreams of a coconut
TA IULI

Will 'Ilolahia didn't give an exact reason for turning up at this urgent meeting at the Auckland University café. Up till then I knew him from sixth form at Mount Albert Grammar but even from that close association, I couldn't speculate on what was going down. Sure enough, it was a very tense situation when I met up with Will, Fred, Nooaroy, Eddie, Vaughan and others; it was too long ago to remember exactly who was there, but I do remember that it was a meeting short on words.

You could sense this anger and frustration seething beneath the grim faces of the young people attending the first day of the formation of the Polynesian Panthers. Being an Islander helped me identify with the group, but I still felt uneasy. I still felt as if I had been called up for military service to a secret strike force dressed in black. On the day there was more than enough muscle on hand. And guns if need be, shotguns at that. And knives, especially machetes, came to mind. Right from the outset I sensed my own inner conflict to the use of militancy and links to the Black Panthers of the United States. The ends might have justified the means in forging the movement, but I just couldn't go along with it.

Within six months I left the Panthers. It would take more than 30 years for me to resolve this issue and I found that resolution in the words of a much-respected human rights campaigner and poet, the late Denise Levertov: 'Now the peace movement must become the revolutionary movement; must work to educate people to the realisation that the struggle of black people *inside* the United States is a struggle for self-determination parallel to those *outside* the United States.' I am sure that if I had a broader understanding of the issues at the time, I would have stayed longer.

Which brings me to my role as minister of information. My mission was to give the perspective of Polynesian youth on acts of racism that besieged not only Pacific communities, but also our Māori brothers and sisters. So to address these racial issues we held a series of meetings at schools and other public venues. It was never a problem fronting up to individuals and groups who listened and asked questions. Nevertheless, that racism existed in New Zealand was always denied with platitudes like: 'Some of my best workers are islanders.' I pretended

---

The Black Panther   September 1974

Polynesian Panther Party Works For Humane Society

---

not to notice the 'bunga' and 'coconut' jokes in the halls and on the buses.

Those taunts echo right back to the playgrounds of my own childhood. Unbeknown to me, there was something even more sinister than those verbal jibes: that is, the institutionalised exclusion of Pacific and Māori peoples by the Pākehā/Palagi. Those days it was so subtle that it left you wondering – what was the point of a young brown person getting an education if you could not even imagine climbing the first rung of the management ladder in the public sector? (Don't even think about the corporate

arena.) For those of us with at least half a brain, the God Ministry was the only way up. For those of us with no hope, the only path was downwards into crime and the gangs.

It wasn't so long ago that Polynesians provided the backbone for manual labour and menial, low-paid work while squatting in Ponsonby. And they still do provide that backbone, but living in suburbs further out. For many, the only relief was the Family Naval, the Rising Sun and the Star Hotel on a packed Thursday night in Karangahape Road, otherwise known as Coconut Grove. Since then, there are those of us who now think that we have evolved beyond that lowly status as beasts of burden: that we have been accepted into the White's Club of fundamentalism. So much so that we can cast stones at homosexuals as if they are a subspecies and deny them their basic right for civil union. How easily we forget the struggles of our own marginalised, migrant forebears and the recriminations from the Dawn Raids.

Looking back again, there is also my recollection of the pitched battle outside Eden Park between the anti-apartheid protesters and the pro-rugby supporters. In my Marlborough Street flat (close to Eden Park) I listened in silence with my young son on his weekend visit. I still wonder if, given the opportunity, I would join the side of the protesters. Not really. How could breaking a few heads and then getting smashed by both Muldoon's pigs and rugby fanatics solve anything? Nevertheless, to this very day, and despite my own rugby roots, I remain embittered by the knowledge that there were those who refused to see the correlation between human rights and rugby rights. These same people condone and ignore the subjugation of the oppressed majority to promote the male bonding, ball-wrenching antics of the few.

Today, it's not any simpler. The lines are blurred; it's not so easy to distinguish black from white or blue from red. Racism has been only one of many obstacles for all Polynesians. When you peel away the layers of racism, social injustice and ignorance, you still end up with more choices and uncertainties:

- How can we sustain ourselves physically, mentally and spiritually?
- How can we break the vicious cycle of family violence and drug abuse?
- What must we do to secure a future for our families and communities?

Aside from trying to meet these new challenges, my aim is to chase the dreams of an unfulfilled youth. Although I never subscribed to the military stance of the Panthers, I have always maintained a kind of physical and mental discipline. It seems such a late time in one's life to return to full-time university study, but the six-kilometre walk every day makes it worthwhile. Every day that I walk, I also remind myself of the debt I owe my mother when she first tried to put me through university in the early 1970s. I can never truly repay her.

Summoning up those memories makes my current hardships seem trivial. They also rejuvenate my focus on my goals. Ultimately, I hope to rediscover the wonders of learning for children, speak my native tongue again and express my forsaken culture through my graphic art. The time has come for me to wake up from a 50-year slumber and bring dreams to reality. The time has also come for the collective conscience of the Polynesian Panthers – which incorporates especially our silent ones – to bring closure and healing to the divisions among us. Let our quest for Polynesian actualisation, including that of our Māori brethren, be a resurrection of our once-forgotten aspirations. Long live the movement.

Tell me my beautiful flying fish
As you soar up to pearly white clouds
As you dive into an emerald coral sea
Am I in paradise or is this just a dream
As I sleep beneath this lazy coconut tree?

My role as a Panther (still)

MELANI ANAE

The Panther experience … has provided me with the passion, skills, knowledge and guts to stand up for what I believe in. To empower my family and Pacific communities, to stand up and fight back, if they are being threatened by the system and/or by inequitable and racist practices. The Panther experience in working with other grass-roots groups has provided me with the nous and strategies to get things done in quick time and has enabled me to see the pragmatism and sense in working with people rather than against them. Above all it has reinforced the value and importance of education as the tool that will lead us out of oppression and darkness and into the light. As a Panther, it is still my role to conscientise and inform and provide pathways as our parents and grandparents did when they forged their journeys to New Zealand and beyond. It is also my role to tell our kids about the importance of our Pacific cultures – the fa'aSamoa – its beauty and its transformations over time and space – in making us who we are. It hasn't been easy. I use, acknowledge and try to maximise both lifeways. I am committed to providing these pathways to other New Zealand-borns who are still negotiating their way/space along their own identity journeys. I am now at peace with myself, those I love, my God and with all others. He aha te mea nui no te ao? He tangata, he tangata, he tangata! Power to the People![1]

Soifua[1]

The great desiderata

ALEC TOLEAFOA

An enduring legacy of my experience as a Panther has been a continuing concern about the issues that affect the well-being of Pacific people. I have carried that concern with me into every sphere of my life, including my vocation as a minister of religion.

The Panthers introduced me to the notion that religion/Christianity was/is being used as a powerful instrument in the colonisation of Pacific nations and peoples.

In the 1960s and 1970s, our urgent needs were tangible and visible and they are to some extent, the same today. The great desiderata at the moment, lies in the recovery of an awareness of our own Pacific spirituality, which has been exorcised by layers and layers of Western religious and cultural world-views since the 1830s.

Spirituality as distinct from religion includes, among other things, an inner awareness of a sacred connectedness to our own spiritual history. I have, for example, a stronger sense of connectedness with Tagaloa a Lagi of the Samoan tradition than I do with Abraham, Isaac and Jacob of the Judaeo-Christian tradition.

In most Pacific world-views, all life is intimately connected to a spiritual dimension, and it is by that connection that all things find value. The incidents of self-harm, domestic violence, alcohol and drug taking, poor mental health, low self-esteem underachievement involving Pacific people are probably indicators of a need to rediscover and reconnect with our own spirituality or at least expose an awareness of it. The Panther experience has given me the tools, the inspiration and passion to continue the process, whether temporal or spiritual, of reclaiming what has always been ours.

Soifua

A time of awareness, a time for change

VAUGHAN SANFT

Basically it was a long time ago. We were a group of guys watching things that were happening around Ponsonby. I believe it was a time of awareness to see what was actually happening with younger people: younger people getting picked up; held in police stations and detained without any sort of advice at all. And the next minute you hear that person is in a borstal or something like that. So we formed a group and tried to change the way things were happening.

I think the older generation had the feeling that eventually it would come right. People of our age weren't that patient. It was time for change and it needed to be done then. I think worldwide this was starting to happen and we were just people of the times.

My role in the Polynesian Panthers was minister of supplies. That involved organising supply casements for things like transport to different march sites or wherever we were going. These are just skills that we learnt and picked up along the way.

I remember we used to attend some of the Ngā Tamatoa meetings. We worked in together, we were both sympathetic to the cause, we both supported each other. I didn't find any flack from the Māori community at all. What I actually found was a lot of support, moral support, and the support was always there; information was also there which helped quite a lot as well.

One of the key events that I organised was one of the marches that actually came down Queen Street here. There were possibly 2000 people. The march was very orderly, even though the police and the traffic police tried to control it. It was my duty to ensure that the march went according to our plans and not theirs. There were people there from all age groups, from different walks of life. There were Polynesian, Māori, Pākehā, which was a good sign of unity.

What we actually noticed was that there were different countries where the natives were also experiencing a lot of difficulty – Aborigines, American Indians, black Americans and other ethnic groups that were being scrutinised around the world

I believe for myself that the main achievement of the Panthers was to make people in New Zealand more aware of what was happening in the political system, also the policing system. For example, the Dawn Raids: nobody likes being woken up at any time in the morning, then thrown out of your bed and marched out the door.

The help the Panthers actually gave me was to understand different cultures and to accept different nationalities. I think it's helped me quite a lot.

At the time I was an apprentice chef. Now I'm an executive chef, working in many different countries in Africa, Asia and the Middle East.[2]

Our contribution to history

TIGILAU NESS

The members of the Panthers have gone on to good things: teachers, lecturers, ministers. I am a musician.

I am in a position of some importance I suppose. I deal with people's radiology. When people are sick then I am the one doing the X-rays. We haven't all been killed off as revolutionaries. Our main aim was then and is still now equality and a more peaceable Aotearoa. So until that happens we will always be going. Haven't died off or changed …

When Bastion Point happened we were ready to take on the Army. There was a military wing of the Panthers. We were ready then … But the land was passive. If people knew what we had there it might have been different. If we had gone the way of the hotheads we could have been different. A big plus for passive resistance. I felt that they [the police] were just doing a job. They weren't all 'pigs'. It was the government. So we thought we'd target the government – the heads. Not the soldiers. Bill Birch, minister of immigration. We had a lot of European people in there to pressure and were able to achieve a lot.

In the Panthers we had a platform that said, 'We are responsible for our own destiny' and thank you very much for helping, but for the Europeans who wanted to join we said, 'Sorry but you have to start your own groups.' So a lot of them did. And we took it all on together. There were some that didn't want white people but usually the people that were best were those trained at university. For myself they [Europeans] were my heroes. Because they didn't have to do it. They had a conscience – Tom Newnham, David Lange, Oliver Sutherland, ACORD. They copped flack: 'nigger lovers'.

We all felt pride in ourselves. There was a choice at the time where you either joined a gang or you got ostracised … We weren't a gang. We were standing up for people. With the self pride, Black Pride, we felt different from gangs. The black leather and beret was quite intimidating. We don't feel like a gang. We weren't a gang. Will would go out to the Otahuhu tavern and hand out pamphlets. Doing it for the people. Got flack. Today people get paid for it.

I liken Agnes Tuisamoa to Eva Rickard and Betty Wark and even Whina Cooper who represented Māori people, but Agnes represented Samoan people. She didn't go for recognition. Had a lot of children. Took on children. If you're born in the Islands then that's your life, but here, she looked after everyone. She was the oldest member of the Polynesian Panthers. She followed her son. He joined: was a bit of a nerd, was in trouble, wanted to help his people … Agnes came along. Mrs Tuisamoa: 'I join the Panthers now. I come to follow my son to make sure he doesn't get in trouble.' We had to listen to her. She was older. She was a stirrer. She helped her son a lot. Wherever we had activities she would be in the background. Never one to take the limelight.

We had no parents who believed in us. My mum: 'Why you go fight for those Māoris for? Why you fight the police?' We got in trouble. Agnes was like other Māori famous women. Her children and grandchildren will reap the benefits. She went all the way to help people. She was the true parent. She was the boss. Wasn't afraid to face authority and stand up for her children. Was a really good ally. Supportive. [For more on the story of Agnes and Vincent Tuisamoa see Part Four.]

Like some who lived in Kingsland, their neighbours, maybe were lucky … Didn't take long to filter out to the rest of the community What could we do for them? When it affected our people it affected all of us. They [young people] have not gone through it and experienced it. If it happened today it would be different. 'Dawn Raid' [a recording company] taking that name has kept it going.

Keeping it in the consciousness. Why Dawn Raid? Because it happened here. It's part of their history.

This is part of the Pacific nation. And all those things like Dawn Raids are part of our history. We have the right to determine our own destiny. Not English. The rest of the migrants who come to live here, there is a certain way of living. Islands are too small to kill people. For Aotearoa, the rest of the world doesn't know about aroha. We have our own way. The reo is still here. In the Cook Islands they own their own land. They don't sell it off. Foreshore business. They own the land. It's different from here. It's big enough to share. No Dawn Raids. It still exists here: racism. I don't know if young people are dumbed down. But through rap it is still there. This is the Pacific. Things are still being forged. It's the mix that is going on. Us being Panthers back then has contributed to history. We don't take things lying down.[3]

My metamorphosis stage
NESS SESEGA

The Panther era was a special time. I reflect back on as my 'metamorphosis' stage. As with many young Polynesians, everyone had a story: a victory, a loss and disappointment. Whatever the big picture – the main events and issues, local and international – and regardless of what the Panthers were about, the movement ignited Pacific youth.

It was a generation that needed a voice, a leader, role models; something to be proud of. Confusion over parents, ideals, values, the fa'aSamoa way and religious issues added to the experience. Being opinionated was termed as back-chatting, leaving no room for expression. Release was through

'Eight arrests at city protest rallies: 3,000 march for Aborigines' Day', in the
Sydney Morning Herald, July 1972, p.3.

sports; singing was a natural talent that was yet to be appreciated except on Sundays when selecting the choir. Violence and gangs were a cry for identity and recognition. Polynesian justice and disciplinary measures were recycled and inherent.

The Panther movement, for some, was a vehicle to reflect one's frustrations; to rebel, violate, and excuse ourselves, blaming the Palagi partly for our short-sightedness. It was easier to dress and look like the 'brothers'; it was harder to grow an afro and connect with parents. Looking back it was a blessed diversion.

One day you realised you were in calmer waters; victory to whoever adjusted and mapped out their lives first. Unless you were doing time, then you were

the next generation. The Black Panther movement in America had an enormous impact on the Polynesian Panthers, and, while the sensitive issues of racism could have been addressed with a more passive approach, it was something that would always regenerate, resurface and recycle itself in a different form.

What was racism to a Samoan youth? I'm as racist today as I was then: eating my Indian brother's lunch. What was prejudice? When I knew he had more but shared it with someone else? I didn't fully understand.

The sacrifice and struggle by our American brothers rallied movements worldwide. We were fortunate not to suffer a similar fate; for some of us, it was a personal triumph to exercise freedom of speech. For others it was 'follow and be captivated' by the hysteria and unity of that nature that was always going to draw attention for the wrong reasons. For my generation, it was a realisation that the world didn't revolve around Ponsonby, Church and social clans. Education is still the only weapon to combat social hostility.

Questionnaire responses from Panthers and Investigators

WHAT WAS YOUR EARLIEST MEMORY OF THE POLYNESIAN PANTHERS?

ALOMA WEHI

My first recollections were of Fred Schmidt (bless his big bear of a heart), he was involved with the Auckland 'Black Panthers'. Fred was the brother of my close friend Etta Schmidt. Fred was holding a meeting in his room at their family home in Keppell Street, Grey Lynn. Etta asked me to attend this meeting, and am unsure of what reason she gave me as to what it was all about … The purpose of the meeting that day was to promote awareness of racism that was present in our daily lives and to do something positive to put a stop to it … this meeting was the inaugural meeting to form the Polynesian Black Panther Movement.

ELIZABETH MEANATA

My earliest memory of the Polynesian Panthers was going to the Baptist Church for a meeting with Aloma, Lucy, Melani, Cherie, sister Mere, Etta, Sally. I was apprehensive at first and felt a little intimidated by the guys, firstly because I did not know them and secondly I was told that some of them were ex gang members. That all changed once I got to know them and learnt more about what the group was about. Thereon in I felt quite protected by our brothers.

SAM SEFUIVA

An urban youth movement from the Auckland inner-city struggles of various street 'gangs' and their desire to create dominance on the streets … A movement which tried to consolidate these groups with common Polynesian ideals and strength against public institutions such as the local Police and initiating housing and education programmes.

SALLY ATIGA

… attending a meeting on a Sunday afternoon at the Baptist Church on the corner of Seymour St and Jervois Rd. Remember telling my dad that Fred and I were joining a Polynesian Youth Group. He didn't seem to mind. Probably thought it was connected to a Church – good move having the inaugural meeting at such a venue!

MAPU IULI

I remember being at Henry Nee Nee's house downstairs. Lots of members, male/female. Sanding back and painting timber houses. Garden work. Delivery of groceries/veges and fruit, orders. Jail transport to and fro. Marches.

MERE MEANATA-MONTGOMERY

Going to a meeting at the Redmond St house in 1971.

HOW DID YOU GET INVOLVED WITH THE PANTHERS?

ALOMA WEHI

I got involved because my friends and I had the same vision.

ELIZABETH MEANATA

I got involved with the Polynesian Panthers through Melani and Lucy as they were at varsity and as we hung out socially, this was an extension of our social scene.

SAM SEFUIVA

Through my cousins and former school friends from Ponsonby/Grey Lynn who wanted support and help on a variety of street initiatives.

SALLY ATIGA

Will kept 'pestering' us at uni – naa! Will talked about setting up a group and invited us from the original 'Cafe Society' to come along: me, Lani, etc.

MAPU IULI

Older brother as you know was involved, being my political mentor. It was inevitable and I couldn't wait to be a part of a local, radical, grass-roots organisation. With an agenda to help the needy in any way possible.

MERE MEANATA-MONTGOMERY

Went along to do the traditional chaperoning or keeping an eye on my younger sister, Elizabeth Meanata (just joking). Largely went because it was Pacific-Island-based group, which appealed to my social conscience. Keep in mind that unbeknownst to my parents, I was parading around in anti-Vietnam demonstrations and the Progressive Movement demos (Tim Shadbolt era), got myself to some interesting meeting which were of similar ilk. (I don't know what my parents thought I was up to, probably thought I was doing good deeds for the Catholic Church through the Legion of Mary!!??) My other excuse was that the St Pat's kids seem to be interested in this and Etta's brother Sam was in it and so was cuzzy Will and I thought it was safe and okay.

LENORA NOBLE

I initially saw an article in the *Sunday News* and it was an article about Will 'Ilolahia and it explained the group and what it was doing and at that time with everything that was happening with a lot of Pacific families, particularly the overstayer issue, and also my own experiences with our Pacific students in schools, I felt that was a group that I would be interested in finding out more about, which I did, and then I consequently joined …[4]

WHO BROUGHT YOU ALONG OR INTRODUCED TO THE POLYNESIAN PANTHERS?

ALOMA WEHI

Etta. (Blame her.)

ELIZABETH MEANATA

I'm pretty sure it was Lucy and Melani that introduced me to the Polynesian Panthers as they were at varsity, and I think Will was kind of bugging them to join the group.

SAM SEFUIVA

My cousin with who our family had been staying with before we moved to our own home in Grey Lynn.

SALLY ATIGA

Will 'Ilolahia – the Man!!

MAPU IULI

Can't truly remember. As I said, it was inevitable: blame it on Ta.

MERE MEANATA-MONTGOMERY

Can't remember but I'm sure I went willing …

ELIZABETH MEANATA

My first impression of the Polynesian Panthers was that it was a youth group and that most of the members were part of a gang and that they were going to do good things within the community. As my sister Mere was with me, Mum thought it was okay and seeing it was just up the road, the girls met at home then up the meeting room in Ponsonby.

The Black Panther   October 1974

Polynesian Panther Party Interview. Liberation Struggle in New Zealand

WHAT DID YOU THINK THE POLYNESIAN PANTHERS WERE ABOUT?

ALOMA WEHI

First off a 'gang' with the Polynesian community in mind. Looking back now – what was the Polynesian Panthers really about? It was about awareness of racism that was present in our lives and how to resolve those issues. It became quite a social movement with the members becoming like brothers and sisters. We learnt from each other's cultures and mores … we respected each other's parents and family values. We learnt from each other how awful and soulless one can be made to feel with racism. We learned how to react to our parents' reaction to our involvement … (many or all were VERY supportive). It made you realise that you had dealt with racism all your lives …

SAM SEFUIVA

A group of friends who were attending 'varsity' wanting to do something different and keeping our young ones from missing out on their education, their families from continually being 'rolled' by dodgy landlords, police, pedantic bureaucrats.

A street movement of inner-city communities wanting to take ownership of their destiny. An opportunity to educate, initiate community actions and instil confidence amongst many Pacific/Māori residing in the inner city; strong, Pacific men and women taking no shit; access to resources that kept our parents in New Zealand and out of jail or on the slow boat back to their homelands; a movement alongside Pacific Youth Movement, Ngā Tamatoa and others.

SALLY ATIGA

Identity, second generation. Lost the lingo. Acceptable 'gang'. Wore cool black berets. Identified and sympathised with American negro struggle – Black Power! Community service.

MAPU IULI

It was a lifetime's opportunity to become personally involved and politically aware. It was unique in that I could give to my community a service in labour and yet I learnt so much about life, politics and what really matters. The above is in hindsight. First impressions were that it must be right in that my brother wanted and was involved as were to be many friends. The similarity in oppressed groups internally didn't escape me. Here was an organisation willing and as able as possible to help and educate.

MERE MEANATA-MONTGOMERY

I was impressed that the Polynesian bros were becoming politically motivated and the Black Panther ideology and programmes sounded great. I was no radical but I was interested in influencing change for our people. I wasn't interested in the guys, cause they were like my brothers, I was only interested in the philosophy (hey, I can spell this now that I have had an edu-ma-cation) and the potential to make changes (why else do you think I have spent so many 'ears doing good for who-man-i-t-e).

LENORA NOBLE

It was what the group was about and I must say that it actually did even educate me further and make me even more politically aware of not just with what was happening in New Zealand but globally, and I don't think I would have been as aware if I hadn't been a part of the group ...[5]

HOW DID IT HELP YOU? POLYNESIAN PEOPLE AND OTHER COMMUNITIES?

ALOMA WEHI

... it turned around my thinking ... it made me think about how my life was going to be lived, and honestly has affected my whole life in these last 30 years. It affected me by being more community-minded, more aware of the underdog ... made me want to achieve in my life the best that I can be. I am the self-appointed 'cultural safety' person in the units I work in, for all cultures. Look out anyone that oversteps the boundaries of common respect. I think it helped the Polynesian community as a whole as we were quite vocal – we were supported by various organisations, which raised the profile of the Polynesians in Auckland.

ELIZABETH MEANATA

Looking back now on the Polynesian Panthers I think it definitely was about identity. Really did raise my awareness on Pacific Island issues. Racial profiling, police and one's rights were something new to me ... In a way it was a turning point for me, in the sense that we were Polynesians helping Polynesians and others within the community.

SAM SEFUIVA

A rallying point for young inner-city Polynesians. Continued encouragement to achieve and recognise one's own identity.

SALLY ATIGA

... Gave our generation something to belong to. Raised our awareness of PI issues. A lovely group of friends ... Personally, I enjoyed meeting and being friends with all involved. We provided some sort of service to the community that wasn't there before ... ran a couple of socials, helped out some old people somewhere along the line ….

MAPU IULI

This was the practical and the theory in action. This was for real! It gave me a sense of worth/value. It gave me political insight as to what can be achieved with the minds and hearts of those who wanted to care. I felt great pride in my community. It made me feel I belonged. Old Ponsonby I miss you and I will never forget you – it's as if we responded to a call at a particular time. It's about helping those at the bottom of the ladder. I painted, cleaned and helped the elderly at home. About delivering a better deal. About strength in solidarity. About providing services at cost or below. Shouldering the costs. About pride in ourselves. About political power and awareness. It was a statement that Polynesian Panthers had a very relevant message for our community, and we were prepared to do something about it.

MERE MEANATA-MONTGOMERY

It kept me focused on my path to social work. Originally wanted to do law, then drifted, via teaching and probation work, to social work.

LENORA NOBLE

I think probably more on a political level being a lot more aware of what was happening not only in New Zealand but also in the world and also being able to pass that on to students …[6]

WHAT WAS YOUR EXPERIENCE WITH THE POLYNESIAN PANTHERS LIKE?

ALOMA WEHI

Good. Being a member of the PPM and being made aware of racial unfairness has made such a huge impact in my life, and I didn't really think of it as being so until the thesis was done on the PPM, which I was interviewed for. It made me think … yes it made such a difference to my life … so I thank you all for that.

ELIZABETH MEANATA

Definitely good – in fact that it raised my awareness of being Polynesian. It was an extension of my immediate social group and also we were involved in doing community work, e.g. homework centres, helping the aged, etc.

SAM SEFUIVA

Good and sometimes indifferent due to the many external influences from the varsity student movements, community action groups, police, burgeoning civil liberties groups and indifferent school attitudes.

SALLY ATIGA

Lovely, thanks! I look back with fondness and much aroha! I remember delivering all those bloody newspapers (*West End News*) all over those hills off Great North Rd to help bring in some revenue.

MAPU IULI

Was it good or what? No, it was fucking great! To this day, my political and moral views moulded with the hand of the Almighty. I pay respects and give many thanks to the experience, life showed me by being involved with the Polynesian Panthers. I believe it made me more mature. The *alofa* that I felt from members I know. I respect greatly those before me who guided and shielded us younger ones, who in their wisdom were brave enough just to create the Polynesian Panthers.

MERE MEANATA-MONTGOMERY

My experience with PPP was positive, the bulk of my experience was in Dunedin.

ANY OTHER COMMENTS?

ELIZABETH MEANATA

Melani, Will, Ta and Lusi, my thanks to you all for energies in putting this book together. Ofa atu.

SAM SEFUIVA

While our parents may not have approved of the more outrageous actions, they approved of the intent that their young were not putting up with the 'crap' that they received when first settling in New Zealand.

SALLY ATIGA

I'll always remember my mum cooking a pot of her yummie chop suey for a social at the Ponsonby Community Centre. At the tail-end of the evening there was some disagreement (needless to say, there had been alcohol invoved!) and one of our usually lovely teddy bears (who else but Eddie!) picked up Mum's empty pot and threw it on the ground…great! How was I going to explain this gigantic dent to my mum?? Anyway, suffice to say, we all survived and that pot still serves wonderful chop suey as a reminder of 'the good times'!! Much alofas!

MAPU IULI

Thank you for the movement. On a personal level, to you Ta, Will, Melani and Lusi, thank you. I am honoured to have had this experience. The timing was right and I believe we had our hearts in the right place.

MERE MEANATA-MONTGOMERY

I know a lot of people talk about PP and Auckland in the same breath, but I'd like to add some info about the Dunedin PP branch [see Part Five].

ENDNOTES

1   Excerpt, with minor editing, from Anae, M. (2003) 'O a'u/I: My Identity Journey'. In Fairbairn Dunlop, P. and Makisi, G. (Eds) *Making Our Place: Growing up PI in New Zealand.* Palmerston North: Dunmore Press.

2   Excerpt from *Panui Pasifika: Protest.* 25 January 2006, Māori Television.

3   *Dawn Raids.* 5 June 2005, TV One. Auckland: Isola Productions.

4   Excerpt from *Panui Pasifika: Protest.* 25 January 2006, Māori Television.

5   Excerpt from *Panui Pasifika: Protest.* 25 January 2006, Māori Television.

6   Excerpt from *Panui Pasifika: Protest.* 25 January 2006, Māori Television.

SHOPPING!
WEEK!
HUGH WRIGHT
FLACKSONS
END POLITE
RACISM
AGAINST
newlynn no hall
newhall no trouble!
HELP US
HELP YOU
REOPEN
DANCE

PART SEVEN

THE LEGACY OF THE POLYNESIAN PANTHERS[1]

"The revolution we openly rap about is one of total change. The revolution is one to liberate us from racism, oppression and capitalism. We see many of our problems of oppression and racism are tools of this society's outlook based on capitalism; hence for total change one must change society altogether." [2]

The infamous persecution of Polynesians in the 1970s, when police and dogs descended on Auckland homes at the crack of dawn, left a bitter legacy for many New Zealanders. The stigma of overstaying tested the resolve and sense of community for Polynesians in New Zealand. The Dawn Raids attacked their collective psyche, touched the core of many Polynesian people and questioned their place in New Zealand. The images, experiences and memories of the Dawn Raids have changed Polynesian perceptions of New Zealand and New Zealanders' perceptions of Polynesians. But as insulting and humiliating as that pivotal chapter in our history has been, all New Zealanders should be touched by the collective, radical action taken by groups such as the Polynesian Panthers and other communities of concerned New Zealanders who ensured that New Zealand's seemingly apartheid immigration policies and police action of the 1970s would never happen again. After all the juggernaut of Polynesian peoples making New Zealand 'their place' cemented by their formidable contributions to New Zealand society at a plethora of levels can never be stopped.

Politically, many are eager to point out that the Dawn Raids and New Zealand's immigration policies in the 1970s were an offshoot of the general malaise felt in New Zealand's relationship with other Pacific countries, especially Samoa and Tonga. New Zealand's immigration policies and harsh treatment of overstayers was hot on the agenda of many an annual South Pacific Forum in the 1970s. It was felt that New Zealand's capitalist actions in the Pacific were self-seeking, based on imperialist ambitions emanating from the United States. An article in New Zealand's socialist newspaper *People's Voice*, 2 August 1976, called for revolution and impelled Pacific people to end this white exploitation, United States' imperialism, and the ruthless imperialism of New Zealand. [3]

Conceptually, the Dawn Raids served two purposes: first, illustrating conditions that made revolution seem necessary; and second with the involvement of Polynesian Panthers, constructing a visual mythology of power for people who felt powerless and victimised. The Panthers worked hard to put an end to the police brutality leading up to and including the Dawn Raids and sought to overcome racist policies which were hindering equitable access to quality education, health, housing and a variety of other social conditions. They did this by working collaboratively with and supporting all people/groups that mirrored their ideals. They also worked hard to liberate Polynesian peoples and communities by demystifying the media's portrayal of power differentials between minority and majority groups. They exposed discrimination by the white press and informed their people about racism in this country.

Even when their formal involvement with the Panthers ended, many members have remained Panthers in terms of their firm commitment to combating all forms of racism – through a variety of strategies – anywhere that they work, play, do business or make music. They continue to share an intense drive to mentor and support Pacific youth

(Top) Panthers protest. From left to right, holding banner one: Wayne Toleafoa, Ariu (Lank) Sio;
banner two: Etta Gillon [née Schmidt], Lenora Tongalea, Janice Taylor, Aloma Ahmu Wehi, Elizabeth Meanata.
(Bottom left) Theresa Ahmu Montgomery, Etta Schmidt Gillon, Eddie Williams.
(Bottom right in foreground) Wayne Toleafoa, Ariu (Lank) Sio.
(Etta Gillon [née Schmidt] archive).

in realising their full potential by drawing on their Pacific cultures and heritages and developing their professional skills as New Zealanders.

In combination, the occupations and activities of all Panther members who tell their stories in this book are committed to elevating Pacific people in the educational, philosophical, secular, spiritual and political spheres, thus removing their status in New Zealand society as second-rate citizens.

It is no accident that so many Panthers are in professions and occupations in which they can initiate social change for Pacific peoples from within the system or act as guardians of Pacific peoples when they brush with the law or misunderstand the bureaucratic structure. Panthers state definitively that their dealings with the system – their personal experiences and their observations of what was happening to their peers and families – are what has provided them with the impetus to seek to change the status quo. This progression from personal experience to professional action is a product of the socio-political and historical context of Pacific peoples growing up in New Zealand in the 1960s and 1970s.

Some Panthers recall how as young Pacific Island school leavers they were actively recruited into government departments to cope with the expanding Pacific population, especially in the urban areas of Auckland and Wellington.

While some went on to become teachers, social workers, chefs, musicians, and youth advocates, others became police officers, academics and church ministers. Those who were able to support and associate with tangata whenua became politically astute and turned these skills towards helping their own Pacific communities. It became an assertion of their own Pacific ethnic identity. Some members went to university, where they became not only intellectually stimulated but also involved in political activities on campus.

For many, the university experience was an opportunity to 'reclaim' their identity – to compare their New Zealand-born identities and Pacific knowledges and belief systems against Palagi intellectual systems and movements. It contributed significantly to their critical analysis of what was happening to, or happening for, Pacific peoples living in New Zealand so that they could understand and put into perspective issues of racism, inequality, feminism, the gay movement, power and knowledge. More importantly, university education helped to explain Panther members' experience and understandings of the subordinate position of Pacific peoples in New Zealand society. Some reacted positively to other movements such as feminism and the gay rights movement, others negatively, but the shared outcome was a deeper insight into what they knew of unequal power relations.

Without a doubt the Polynesian Panthers started the revolution for recognition of the burgeoning Pacific presence in New Zealand and the browning of New Zealand of the future. They did all this as 17–19 year olds and were recognised not only by our Pacific communities, but also by the Government of New Zealand and the Black Panthers USA for their work.

In retrospect, it is clear that the Panthers were not a terrorist threat. It does not matter whether the Panthers intended to wage a large-scale retaliatory attack against perceived agents of oppression such as Police, immigration officials, politicians and western ideology. The Dawn Raids and the Panthers call to revolution, in the form of the exposure and annihilation of all forms of oppression, the focus on education, working collaboratively for positive outcomes and mana Pasifika – the celebration of Pacific identities and ethnicities, survives as a lasting vision of empowerment. Without the Dawn Raids, the Polynesian Panthers would not have been able to give 'all power to the people'.

ENDNOTES

1   Excerpt from Anae, M. (2012) 'All Power to the People: Overstayers, the Dawn Raids and the Polynesian Panthers'. In Mallon, S., Mahina-Tuai, K. and Salesa, D. (Eds) *Tangata o le Moana: New Zealand and the People of the Pacific*. Wellington: Te Papa Press, pp.221–240.

2   Polynesian Panther Party (1975) 'What We Want'. In Levine, S. (Ed) *New Zealand Politics: A Reader*. Melbourne: Cheshire, p.226.

3   See Joris de Bres interview in *Dawn Raids*. 5 June 2005, TV One. Auckland: Isola Productions.

New Zealand Panther Movement programme, September 1971

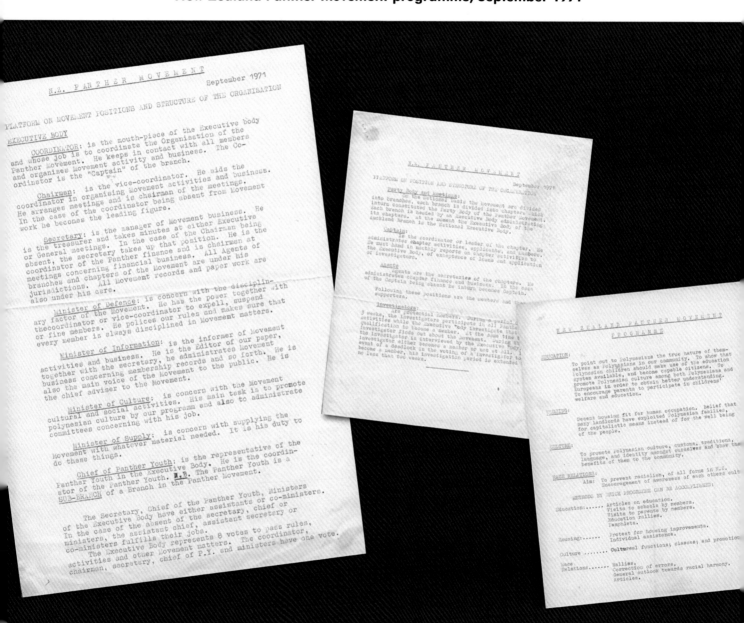

N.Z. PANTHER MOVEMENT   September 1971

PLATFORM OR MOVEMENT POSITIONS AND STRUCTURE OF THE ORGANISATION

EXECUTIVE BODY

COORDINATOR: is the mouth-piece of the Executive body and whose job is to coordinate the Organisation of the Panther Movement. He keeps in contact with all members and organises Movement activity and business. The Co-ordinator is the "Captain" of the branch.

Chairman: is the vice-coordinator. He aids the coordinator in organising Movement activities and business. He arranges meetings and is chairman of the meetings. In the case of the coordinator being absent from Movement work he becomes the leading figure.

Secretary: is the manager of Movement business. He is the treasurer and takes minutes at either Executive or General meetings. In the case of the Chairman being absent, the secretary takes up that position. He is chairman at coordinator of the Panther finance and is chairman of meetings concerning financial business. All Agents of branches and chapters of the Movement are under his jurisdictions. All Movement records and paper work are also under his care.

Minister of Defence: is concern with the disciplin-ary factor of the Movement. He has the power together with the coordinator or vice-coordinator to expel, suspend or fine members. He polices our rules and makes sure that every member is always disciplined in Movement matters.

Minister of Information: is the informer of Movement activities and business. He is the Editor of our paper, together with the secretary, he administrates Movement business concerning membership records and so forth. He is also the main voice of the Movement to the public. He is the chief adviser to the Movement.

Minister of Culture: is concern with the Movement cultural and social activities. His main task is to promote polynesian culture by our program and also to administrate committees concerning with his job.

Minister of Supply: is concern with supplying the Movement with whatever material needed. It is his duty to do these things.

Chief of Panther Youth: is the representative of the Panther Youth in the Executive Body. He is the coordin-ator of the Panther Youth. N.B. The Panther Youth is a SUB-BRANCH of a Branch in the Panther Movement.

The Secretary, Chief of the Panther Youth, Ministers of the Executive Body have either assistants or co-ministers. In the case of the absent of the secretary, chief or ministers, the assistant chief, assistant secretary or co-ministers fulfills their jobs. The coordinator, The Executive Body represents 8 votes to pass rules, activities and other Movement matters. The coordinator, chairman, secretary, chief of P.Y. and ministers have one vote.

N.Z. PANTHER MOVEMENT

PLATFORM ON POSITION AND STRUCTURE OF THE ORGANISATION
                                         September 1971

Party Body and Meetings:
On the National basis the Movement are divided into branches, each branch is divided into chapters which inturn constituted the Party Body of the Panther Movement. Each branch is headed by an Executive Body administrating its chapters. At the moment the Executive Body of the Auckland Branch is the National Executive Body.

Captain:
is the coordinator or leader of the chapter. He administrates chapter activities, applicants, and members. He must hand in monthly reports on chapter activities to the Executive Body, of exceptance or loans and application of investigators.

Agents
Agents are the secretaries of the chapters. He administrates chapter finance and business. In the case of the Captain being absent he inturn becomes Captain.

Following these positions are the members and the supporters.

Investigators:
are protestal members. Durring a period of 3 weeks, the investigators participate in all Panther activities while become Executive body investigate that qualification to become a member. At the same time the investigator finds out about the Movement. During the investigator is interviewed by the Executive Body. In event of a deadlock in the voting of a investigator to become a member, his investigation period is extended to no less than two weeks.

NEW ZEALAND PANTHER MOVEMENT
PROGRAMME

EDUCATION:
To point out to Polynesians the true nature of them-selves as Polynesians in our community. To show that Polynesian children should make use of the education system available, and become capable citizens. To promote Polynesian culture among both Polynesians and Europeans in order to obtain better understanding. To encourage parents to participate in childrens' welfare and education.

HOUSING:
Decent housing fit for human occupation. Belief that many landlords have exploited Polynesian families for capitalistic means instead of for the well being of the people.

CULTURE:
To promote Polynesian culture, customs, traditions, language, and identity amongst ourselves and show the benefits of them to the community.

RACE RELATIONS:
Aim: To prevent racialism, of all forms in N.Z. Encouragement of awareness of each others cult

METHODS BY WHICH PROGRAMME CAN BE ACCOMPLISHED:

Education:...... Articles on education.
Visits to schools by members.
Visits to parents by members.
Education rallies.
Pamphlets.

Housing:....... Protest for housing improvements.
Individual assistance.

Culture .... Cultureal functions; classes; and promotion

Race
Relations........ Rallies.
Correction of errors.
General outlook towards racial harmony.
Articles.

Polynesian Panther Party Legal Aid booklet

N.Z. PAMPHLETS
79-7

LEGAL-AID

POLYNESIAN PANT[HER]

CENTRAL HEADQUARTERS
315 PONSONBY ROAD,
AUCKLAND 2.
PHONE 764-830.

- **A**WHINA A TE TURE
- **F**ESOANI FA'A LE TULAFONO
- **T**AUTURU NO TE PAE TURU
- **L**AGAOMATAI HE FAKATUFONO
- **T**OKONI FAKALAO

P O L Y N E S I A N   P A N T H E R   P A R T Y

L E G A L   A I D   B O O K

<u>INDEX</u>

INTRODUCTION. . . . . Page 1.
Legal Aid on the Street. . . . . Page 3.
Legal Aid at the Station. . . . . Page 6.
Legal Aid in the Courts. . . . . Page 8.
Copies of SEARCH WARRANT

       SUMMONS TO DEFENDANT

       BAIL BOND. . . . . .Centre Pages.
Legal Aid at Home(with the landlord). . Page 9.

       (as an owner). . . . . Page 10.

       (search your home). . .Page 12.
SUMMARY. . . . . .Page 14.

_____

    This book is for your use. Read it over and
over so you know your legal rights.

              ALL POWER TO THE PEOPLE.

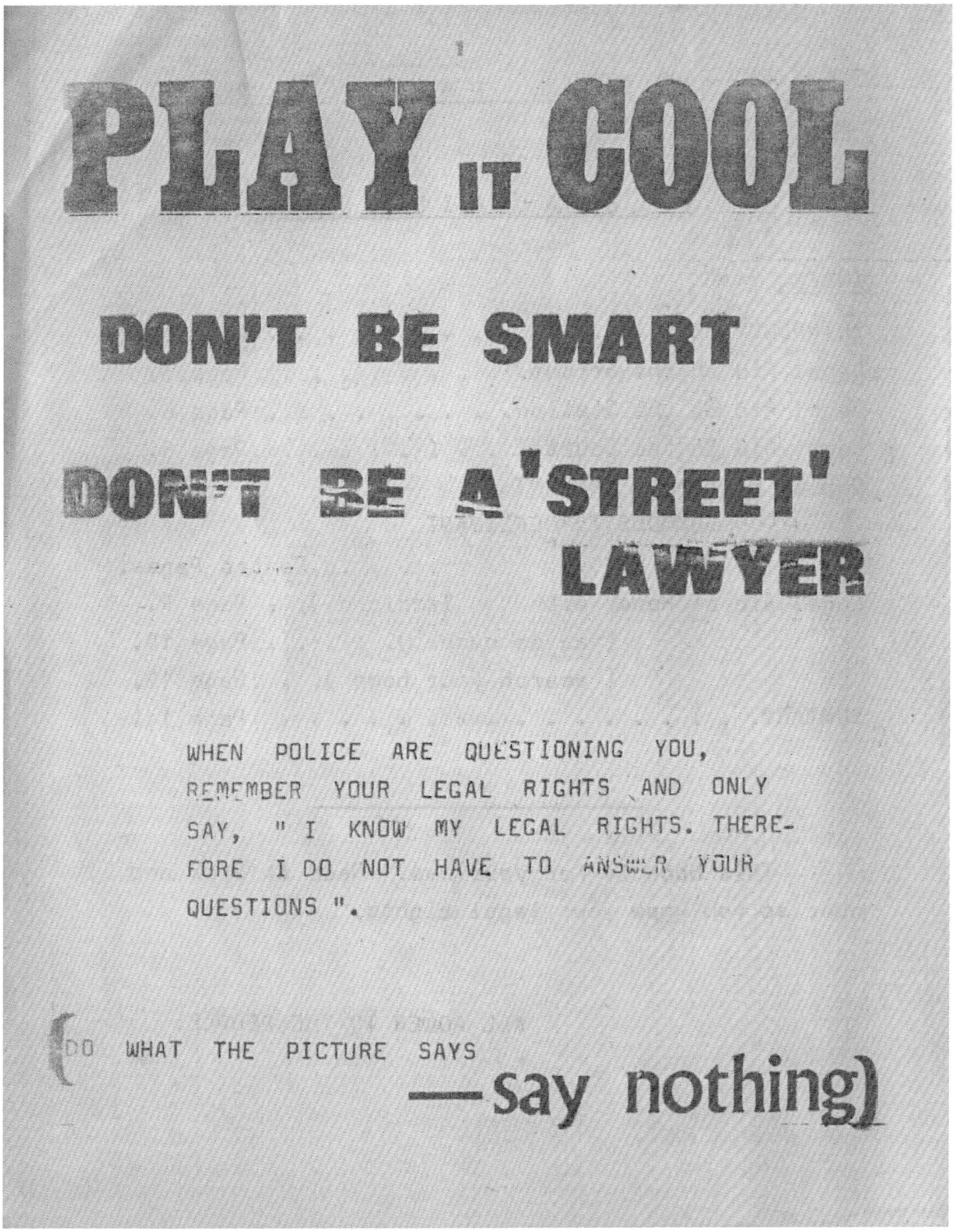

PLAY IT COOL

DON'T BE SMART

DON'T BE A 'STREET' LAWYER

WHEN POLICE ARE QUESTIONING YOU, REMEMBER YOUR LEGAL RIGHTS AND ONLY SAY, " I KNOW MY LEGAL RIGHTS. THEREFORE I DO NOT HAVE TO ANSWER YOUR QUESTIONS ".

(DO WHAT THE PICTURE SAYS —say nothing)

Legal Aid ON THE STREET.

1) If questioned by a policeman, Do Not go with him!
   Always stay with friends. Remember, no law says
   you must answer the police officer's questions!

2) If questioned by a policeman, your only answer
   should be, "I know my legal right,therefore, I do
   not have to answer your questions."
   There is no law that says you must give your name
   and address, except; 1) If you have been arrested!
   2) If you are driving a car!
   on Race course + Pub.
   T.A.B.

3) ARREST; If arrested by a policeman, ask the police
   man if you have been arrested. If the answer is
   "yes", then ask him "on what charge". Never get
   into a police car if not arrested. Only go if
   arrested. Go quietly - otherwise they might add
   more charges.
          Note: If a policeman arrests you unlaw-
   fully, you can try for damages later (wrongful
   arrest)

4) The police do not have to show you a warrant when
   arresting you, but must tell you what they are
   arresting you for. If there is a formal warrant
   out for your arrest then they should show you as
   soon as practicable.

5) <u>SEARCH</u>; the police have no power to search you
   your bags unless; 1) You are on or near a wharf.
                     2) They are searching for drug
                        under the Narcotics act.
                     3) They are searching for guns
                        under the Fire Arms Act.

                 Under arrest

6) If the police search you or your property withou
   permission; 1) Note his number and also ask for
                  his name.
               2) Note his rank(Constable, Corporal,
                  etc.) Police officers above the rank
                  of Sergeant have no number.
               3) If he is a detective(Demons), demand
                  to know his name or to see his I.D
                  card. Remember his description, the
                  plate of police car and the time he
                  was searching you.

Report this to your lawyer, or go to the station
and make a formal complaint, or ring Panther Headquarters (ph 764830).

7) <u>IDLE AND DISORDERLY (I AND D)</u> This does not mean
   what it says. The police are not trying to prove
   that you are idle and disorderly or unemployed,but
   that you have "insufficient lawful means of support".

          If you are supported by parents, rel-
   atives, or friends, you cannot be convicted and
   should plead NOT GUILTY.

          If you are working, again the charge

will not succeed.

  <u>Do Not</u> admit to not having a place to live, or names of friends or relatives who assist you.

8) <u>OFFENSIVE WEAPON</u>; (does not have to be only a fire-arm. A spanner for example can be an offensive weapon, if possessed or used in the wrong way or place). Got to have a good reason for having it, e.g. Travelling with a gun to go shooting or hunting (animals or birds).

  Keep car tools wrapped in a sack or in a tool-box in the <u>boot</u>. Do Not have car tools or other things like that inside the car.

9) <u>Never</u> accept the advice of a policeman on how serious the charge is. Only a lawyer will give you a straight answer. The police may try and talk you in-to giving information or signing a statement. Do Not talk or sign.

<u>Police power</u>. The police have a lot of power. The police and courts work together. So all that can be really done is to be calm, polite and <u>SAY AS LITTLE AS POSSIBLE</u> in regard to the charge. In other words say nothing about the charge and do not be smart!

10) Beware of Bluffs, tricks or slys!!

Any threat, promise, or bargain made by the police to get a statement from you is illegal.

Watch out for the "friendly" policeman. Don't talk to them, because this is one way of them getting evidence. Sometimes they would twist or change what you say to support their case.

11) Private Security men have no power outside the area they are bouncing.

Legal Aid AT THE POLICE STATION.

1) At the station, after being arrested, give name, address and occupation only. Nothing else!!! Do Not give name or place of work because they usually check up.
2) The police are allowed to take fingerprints and photos. Do Not give them prints unless you have been arrested. (Police Act 1958, Section 57)
3) Demand you right to use the phone. Ring your Lawyer, or your relatives, or your friends.
4) Your right to bail; 1. Demand bail as soon as arrested.

2. If the police agree, they will bail you to appear in Court the next day and will probably ask for someone to guarantee (a

surety) that you turn up. You and the surety (who
could be a relative) do not have to have the money
at the station. But the surety may have to show
the police that he or she has $100 (or whatever
the sum). By this, the surety can show a bank-
book or other papers to prove that he or she has
the sum.

3. The police are not comp-
elled to bail you. But if they refuse, you have
the right to be brought before a court (specially
set up if necessary). Contact your lawyer about
this.

4. If you are charged with an
offence punishable by not more than 3 years imprisonment and you have not been charged on an
offence punishable by imprisonment, you have the
legal right to be bailed.

IF THE POLICE DO NOT BAIL YOU THE MAGISTRATE WILL.

5. The police have to bail
you if you are to appear in court within the next
7 days (not Sunday).

5) Demand to see your lawyer, and DO NOT sign anything until your lawyer says it is O.K.

6) You can talk privately with a lawyer (out of
hearing distance from the police).
You can talk with relatives, but not privately.

7) On Line Up - Never co-operate. Never answer

questions. Do Not speak into the microphone.

8) <u>Remember</u> - Insist on; 1. RIGHT TO CONTACT LAWYER.

                    2. RIGHT TO HAVE BAIL.

                    3. RIGHT TO HAVE MEDICAL AID
                       IF NEEDED.

                    4. RIGHT TO HAVE RELATIVES
                       INFORMED.

CONTACTS :

        Polynesian Panther Party
        Central Headquarters   ph. 764 830

        Youthline   73 171

        Resistance   75 693

        Civil Liberties   696 710

        Peoples Union   765 231

<u>Legal Aid IN THE COURTS.</u>

1) <u>IN COURT IF YOU DO NOT HAVE A LAWYER.</u>

      1) You should <u>not</u> plead to a charge
until you have seen a lawyer. Say to the Magistrate, "I WANT TO SEE A LAWYER AND DO NOT WISH TO
ENTER A PLEA UNTIL I HAVE".

      2) You should ask for bail.

      3) Apply for Legal Aid as soon as you
can. Ask the Magistrate for Legal Aid if you have
no lawyer.

      4) Contact Panther Community Worker

Section 198   (S.P.-50)

S E A R C H   W A R R A N T

Summary Proceedings Act 1957

C.R.No:

To: Every Constable

I am satisfied on an application

    *(in writing made on oath)

    *(made on oath orally, the grounds for which I have
      noted in writing)

That there is reasonable ground for believing that there is (are)
in (1) A building, to wit, a dwelling house, situate at _____ ⊛
_____and occupied by _____

the following thing(s) namely: _____ ⊛
_____

*(upon or in respect of which an offence of (2)_____ being an   ⊛
offence punishable by imprisonment   has been or is suspected
of having been committed).

*(which there is reasonable ground to believe will be evidence as
to the commission of an offence of (2)).

*(which there is reasonable ground to believe it is intended to be
used for the purpose of committing an offence of (2))

                                                                  ⊛

THIS IS TO AUTHORISE YOU at any time or times within one month
from the date of this warrant to enter into and search the said
Building with such assistants as may be necessary, and if
necessary to use force for making entry, whether by breaking
open doors or otherwise, and also to break open the *(box)
(receptacle) (any box or receptacle therein or thereon) by force
if necessary; and also to seize.

    *(any thing upon or in respect of which such an offence
      has been or is suspected of having been committed)

    *(any thing which there is reasonable ground to believe
      will be evidence as to the commission of such an offence)

    *(any thing which there is reasonable ground to believe
      is intended to be used for the purpose of committing
      such an offence).

Dated at AUCKLAND this_____day of_____19____ ⊛

                              Magistrate.
                              Justice of the Peace
                              (Deputy) Registrar (not being
                                              a constable).

Note:- _____ ⊛ Special attention should be made to these parts.
                 Question the police if you are not sure of these
                 parts.

BAIL BOND

(Summary Proceedings Act 1957, s. 51 and 52)

DEFENDANT: _____
(Full name)

of _____
(Residence)

_____
(Occupation)

WHEREAS the defendant having been arrested without warrant is charged with_____

_____, being an offence punishable on summary conviction, I the defendant

bind myself to attend personally at the Magistrate's Court at_____ on

_____ day the_____ day of_____ 19___ at_____ a.m.

to answer to the charge, and acknowledge myself bound to forfeit to the Crown the sum of £_____,

in the event that I fail to attend as required by this bond.

_____
Defendant.

*AND I, _____
(Full name)
*Delete if no surety required.

of _____
(Residence).

_____
(Occupation)

AGREE to act as surety and acknowledge myself bound to forfeit to the Crown the sum of £_____

in the event that the defendant fails to attend as required by this bond.

_____
Surety.

SIGNED by the defendant †(and the surety) on the_____ day of_____ 19___
†Delete if no surety required.

in my presence and the sum of £_____ deposited with me.

_____
Constable.

Amount of deposit: £   :   s.   d.

How disposed of_____

Received from the Police Department on_____ the sum of £   :   s.   d. being

the sum deposited by me less the amount of £   :   s.   d. for fine and costs.

_____
Defendant.

This form is subject to revision.

SUMMONS TO DEFENDANT

Set out name and address
of Defendant in postal
address form.

Defendant

Age:

Occupation:

Nationality:
(if arrest)

(1) Full name.

(1)

(2) Address and
occupation.

of (2)   has stated

on oath   that   (*he has just cause to suspect and does suspect that)

YOU the said (1)

*Delete if complaint

(*within the space of   months last past, namely,) on the

day of   19   , at

(3) Here set out sub-
stance of offence, or
matter of complaint.

(3)

*being an offence punishable summarily.

_____
(Here add section and statute applicable)

YOU are summoned to appear

on   day, the   day of   19   , at   a.m.
                                                                                          p.m.

at the Magistrate's Court at   to answer to the information.

Dated at   this   day of   19

_____
Justice of the Peace,
Deputy Registrar (not being a constable)

NOTE: IF YOU SHOULD WRITE TO THE REGISTRAR ABOUT THIS CASE, PLEASE
QUOTE THE NAME OF THE PROSECUTOR AND THE DATE OF HEARING.

137

(Sister Ama Rauhihi), who will be at the courts, or
ring Panther Headquarters phone 764 830.

2) In criminal cases you apply for aid under the
   <u>Offenders Legal Aid Act 1954</u>. Forms are available
   at the courts and Prisons. Welfare officers, Chap-
   lains and probation officers can help you apply
   for Legal Aid.

3) Under the "Legal Aid" system you do not have the
   <u>Right</u> to choose your own lawyer, but the Court may
   take your wishes into account.

4) "Legal Aid" pays the solicitor (lawyer). You may
   have to pay some part of the money, but it depends
   on if you can. If you have the money and have a
   lawyer, you will probably not be allowed "Legal
   Aid".

5) Civil legal aid is quite different and is not for
   cases where the police arrest you, e.g. Divorce
   cases, or breach of promise of marriage.

<u>Legal Aid AT HOME</u>.

<u>WITH THE LANDLORD</u>.

1) Always make a written agreement, which you and the
   landlord would sign. Final agreement should be
   made with the owner not the land agent.

2) An agreement should say how much notice the land-

lord must give you before you leave. For security demand that the agreement gives you a state period, i.e. 6 months.

3) If you have a written agreement, the landlord can only tell you to leave only if you have broken the agreement.

4) If you have NO written agreement, the landlord can tell you to leave for any reason or for no reason at all.

5) If you have NO written agreement, the period of notice depends on what amount you pay for your rent.

> If you pay rent per week - 1 week's notice.

> If you pay rent per month - 1 month's notice.

6) The landlord cannot forcibly throw you out from his flat or house of rent. He must seek a court order. The Court Baliff can throw you out, but he must show you tne Court Order.

7) If you have a written agreement, the landlord can enter to fix something, check the house to see if it is in good condition, and collect the rent. Otherwise you can treat him like a visitor. This is your right as a tenant.

AS A OWNER

8) Strictly speaking no one is allowed to enter your property unless they have been invited.

9) Even the POLICE cannot enter unless you invite them and they must leave, if you tell them to.

Otherwise they can enter only when :

   1. If they have reason to believe that a serious crime has been committed on your property.

   2. They have a search warrant. (Must show warrant if you ask to see it.)

   3. If they believe you have drugs on the property.

   4. If they believe you have firearms on the property.

10) You can call the police to arrest a person who you do not want on your property. (They can be fined up to $200 or 3 months jail.)

11) Repossession Agents can enter your house to take back whatever goods you have not kept up the payments on. But they are not allowed to break in or damage your property, or use rough methods against you.

   Usually, the hire-purchase agreement you sign has a clause which gives them the ri right to enter your property. You can withdraw this right by giving the company notice warning them not to enter the property.

SEARCH YOUR HOME.

12) Never let the police in your house unless :

    1. They have a warrant. Make sure you read it! (Copy of a warrant in middle section of this book.)

    <u>OR</u> 2. When they have legal rights to enter your house without a warrant. This is when:

    a) They can under the <u>Narcotics Act</u> - They must have reasonable grounds to suspect drugs in your home; <u>THEY MUST IDENTIFY THEMSELVES</u> and say what they are there for. Detectives must produce evidence to prove he is a policeman.

    b) They can enter under the <u>Arms Act (1958)</u> - They can enter if they have reasonable grounds to suspect, that anyone at your house has a firearm, and the person is of unsound mind or drunk, or may kill or injure.

    c) They can enter if they are freshly pursuing an offender.

    d) They can enter on grounds to suspect a person will commit a crime, or an offence is committed which will likely cause serious injury to person or property, e.g. a fight or murder. They can use force.

<u>IF THIS HAPPENS, CONTACT A LAWYER AS SOON AS POSSIBLE</u>

13) <u>Warrants</u>. Under the Arms Act, the warrant can only be signed by a commissioner officer (rank of Inspector and upwards.)

"Ordinary" search warrants can only be signed by a Magistrate, a Justice of the Peace or the Registrar.

14) Watch all the police, if they enter. It is vital that every policeman is watched in case they try to plant things such as, papers, drugs, or guns.

15) MAKE SURE YOU READ THE WARRANT AND IDENTIFICATION CARDS OF POLICE OFFICERS.

If you feel that your landlord is charging high rents or is not fixing any damages you have in your flat, contact your lawyer or us,

Polynesian Panther Party
Central Headquarters,
315 Ponsonby Road,
Auckland 1.
Phone 764 830.

If the police have entered your property unlawfully or harass you, contact your lawyer or us.

SUMMARY

LEGAL AID ON THE STREET

Do not try and be smart. PLAY IT COOL. Do not say anything other than, "Iknow my legal right, therefore, I do not have to answer your questions". If arrested go quietly. Beware of bluffs tricks and the "friendly" policeman.

Only enter a police car if arrested.

If you are giving legal aid to another person, note everything that is happening. Do not obstruct the police, but play it cool. Tell the person his or her legal rights. Then ring us or a lawyer. Go to the police station and help him or her get bail. Contact his or her parents.

LEGAL AID AT THE STATION

Do not sign anything until you see a lawyer. Ask for bail and demand your right to contact lawyer or relatives. Give name and address only.

LEGAL AID IN THE COURTS

Do not plead until you have seen a lawyer. Say, "I want to see a lawyer and do not wish to enter a plea until I have".

If you need aid, apply for Legal Aid.

LEGAL AID AT HOME

Always have a written agreement with landlord. If no written agreement, landlord has the power.

Do not allow police to enter, only when they are looking for drugs, guns, criminals, or have a search warrant. Make sure the police identify themselves and watch them in case they plant something in your house.

———————————

NOTES – ADDITIONAL INFORMATION

GLOSSARY

'AIGA family, extended family, descent group or kinship in all its dimensions; transnational corporation of kin

ALOFA love

AOTEAROA (Māori) lit. 'land of the long white cloud', New Zealand

AROHA (Māori) love

A'U I, me

EKALESIA church congregation

FA'AALOALO courtesy, respect, honours, regard highly and treat with respect

FA'ALAVELAVE a ceremonial occasion (weddings, funerals, etc.) requiring the exchange of gifts, anything which interferes with 'normal' life and calls for special activity

FA'ALUPEGA a formal expression of recognition associated with a matai title. Each village and district has a set of fa'alupega, which acts as a constitution by expressing the rank and by alluding to the historical/genealogical origins of the senior titles

FA'AMAULALO (FA'AMAUALALO) to be humble, to humble oneself, be low, be subservient to, to act below one's station

FA'AMAUALUGA proud, to be high, conceited, to act above one's station

FA'APALAGI European ways, like a European, according to the ideas/customs of Europeans

FA'ASAMOA in the manner of Samoans, the Samoan way; according to Samoan customs and traditions

FALE house, traditional house

FEAGAIGA covenant between a brother/sister and their descendants, currently used to refer to covenant between minister/congregation; a contract

FIA want to ...

FIAPALAGI ape the ways and manners of Europeans

GAFA genealogy

HUI meeting, gathering

KAUPAPA (Māori) foundation, earth floor or roots

KOMIKI committee

KU'I (OR TU'I) smash/hit, usually with fist

LAVALAVA clothes; put on, wear 'ie lavalava; also 'ie sulusulu (carelessly wrapped), 'ie solosolo (cloth with floral design), cotton wrap-around, worn like a skirt

MALAE open space in the middle of a village green; area of high social importance

GLOSSARY

MALAGA to visit, a visiting party, visiting 'aiga, ceremonial visit paid according to Samoan custom; journey

MASI biscuits, usually tins of the Cabin Bread type for ritual exchanges

MATAI political representative of 'aiga who holds a title bestowed by 'aiga, custodian of 'aiga land and property. There are two orders of matai – ali'i and tulafale

MAULI Māori

MOSO'OI tall tree with sweet-scented flowers used for scenting coconut oil

NU'U a polity or village, also gu'u

OFU ELEI formal or 'nice' clothes

PA'EPA'E white

PALAGI (PAPALAGI) lit. sky-breaker, white man, Europeans, foreigner, Samoan not born in Samoa (in thesis context)

PALUSAMI dish made with taro leaves, coconut cream and seawater

PATI PATI clapping

PEA like (as opposed to pe'a – tattoo)

PESE song or hymn

PISUPO corned beef

PULETASI 'pair' female formal dress consisting of matching lavalava and dress

SAPASUI chop suey (Samoan style) – dish made with diced meat and chinese noodles/water/soy sauce/salt/onions

SAPO LE MASINA lit. 'catch the moon', any activity under moonlight

SAKA boiled taro

TAMA child; tamā – father. In this context the latter

TAONGA (Māori) treasures – tangible examples include heirlooms and artefacts, land, fisheries, natural resources such as geothermal springs and access to natural resources, such as riparian water rights and access to the riparian zone of rivers or streams; intangible examples may include language, spiritual beliefs and radio frequencies

TAUTUA (of untitled men and other dependants) serve a matai, carry out orders of; those who stand behind those in authority

TINA mother

TOA warrior

TO'ONA'I main Sunday meal

UMU earth oven, food cooked over heated stones

USITA'I to listen; discipline

VA referring to the distance/position of two people/places/things in relation to each other/their relationship, separate yet closely connected

VALEA silly/mad/stupid

WAKA (Māori) canoe

WHAKAMĀ (Māori) shy

COLLOQUIAL WORDS/PHRASES

BLUE gang slang for fracas or fight

BOUSS slang for mate, buddy or friend

BRO, BROS short for brother/brothers

FA, SOLE (abbr.) 'See you, mate'

KIA ORA (Māori) 'Hello' or in some contexts, 'Amen to that'

NICK slang for prison

SPIEL talk or palaver

TANGATA WHENUA (Māori) 'People of the land', Māori peoples

TY too young or teenagers

VA FEALOALOA'I the relationships of mutual respect in socio-political and spiritual arrangements

GLOSSARY

LIST OF ABBREVIATIONS

ACORD Auckland Committee on Racism and Discrimination

BPP Black Panther Party

CARE Citizens' Association for Racial Equality

FOB Fresh Off the Boat; also 'freshie'

HART Halt All Racist Tours

K'RD Karangahape Road

PPM Polynesian Panther Movement

PPP Polynesian Panther Party

MAGS Mt. Albert Grammar School

NLO The Grey Lynn Neighbourhood Law Office

PI Pacific Islander(s)

PIC Pacific Islanders' Church

PICC Pacific Islanders' Congregational Church

PIG Police Investigation Group

PIPC Pacific Islanders' Presbyterian Church

SCHOOL C School Certificate

TECH. Technical Institute

TROPICS ESG missionary outreach programme

UE University Entrance

UNI. University

ABOUT THE EDITORS

Misatauveve Dr Melani Anae joined the Polynesian Panthers in 1971. She is now Senior Lecturer in Pacific Studies at the University of Auckland, is a mother of three and grandmother, and still lives in Ponsonby.

Lautofa (Ta) Iuli was one of the founding Polynesian Panthers. Currently a teacher, his ultimate goal is to make a contribution not just in teaching but in the study of accentuated educational processes.

Leilani Tamu is a New Zealand-born Samoan and was born and bred in Auckland. It wasn't until attending university that she came to fully understand and appreciate the huge impact that they have had on forging the way forward for young PIs. She is now a mother of two children and author of *The Art of Excavation* (Anahera Press 2014). 'I am so grateful to Melani, Ta and Will for giving me the privilege of helping to ensure that their voices are heard.'

INDEX

Ali, Muhammad 89

Anae, Melani 15–22, 29–30, 56, 68, 94, 106, 111, 112, 116

Apaches vi, 65

Apia 4, 21, 22

Atiga, Sally xvi, 111–116

Attwood, Darryl 9

Auckland vi–xii, xiii–xiv, xviii, xix, 4, 5, 23, 24–25, 28, 29–30, 35, 49, 51, 60–62, 68, 72, 91, 96, 100, 108, 111, 114
      see also South Auckland; West Auckland; names of suburbs

Auckland City Council vi, ix, xii, 48

Auckland Committee on Racism and Discrimination (ACORD) xi, 76, 108

Auckland Girls' Grammar School 5, 29, 37

Australia viii, xiii, 48, 50, 62, 89, 93, 102, 104

Avondale vii, 77, 104

Awatere, Donna 82

Bastion Point 48, 60, 66, 101, 102, 104, 108

Baxter, J.K. 93

Beachhaven 30

Beck, Reverend 65

Bhana, Nigel xvi, 59, 60–67, 81

Birch, Bill 59, 108

Birkdale 30

Black Panther movement xi, xiii–xiv, xvi, xviii, xix, 36, 40, 50, 56, 62, 77, 78, 83, 90, 94, 101, 104, 110, 122

Brown, Robert 65

Buchan, Johnny 9

Captain Fred (Fred Schmidt) xvii, 38, 52, 67, 68, 69, 104, 111

Ché Fu 71, 101, 104

China x

Christchurch ix, 48, 54, 61, 91

Citizens' Association for Racial Equality (CARE) 71, 78, 80, 82, 88

Clark, Helen 52

Cleaver, Eldridge xiv, 56

Cook Islands 49, 109

Cooper, Dame Whina 59, 109

Cox's Creek 7, 31

Davies, Piers 76, 77

Davis, Angela 79, 91

De Bres, Joris xvi, 52, 80–82, 88, 122

Dearlove, John 9

Doherty, Lyn 56, 71

Dunedin x, 48, 96–97, 116

Edwards, Sandy xvii, 96

Ellis, Fred 76

Elms, Rodney 9

Fonoti, Tony xvi, 24, 70

Foof (Fa'amoana John Luafutu) xvi, 3–11, 30–44,

Fowler, Roger xvi, xvii, 52, 57, 63, 69, 71, 77, 79, 83

Freeman's Bay 5

Germany x, 93

Gill, Frank 82

Gillon, Etta (née Schmidt) xvi, 57, 66, 67, 121

Glen Innes 30, 59, 77

Grey Lynn vii, 4, 5, 7, 9, 30, 32, 35, 36, 40, 41, 43, 44, 53, 59, 63, 65, 77, 83, 96, 97, 111, 113, 150

Grey Lynn Neighbourhood Law Office 77, 88, 150

Grey Lynn Primary School 5, 11

Grymes, Rick 65

Guttenbeil, Gus 25

Halt All Racist Tours (HART) 49, 150

Harawira, Hone xvi, 82

Harawira , Titiwhai 93

Harris, John xvi

Hart, John 72

Hawke, Joe 62

He Taua 59, 83–84

Head Hunters vii, 49, 64

Helu, Futa 91, 93

Henderson 30, 64, 65

Herbs 66, 102, 104

Herne Bay 7, 30, 39

Hillary College viii

Hilliard, David xiii–xiv

Hodges, Tom xvii, 93

Hola, Sefo ix

Hona, Willie 55

Howick

Hucker, Bruce 101

Hunter, Keith (Jock the Maori) 7

'Ilolahia, Will vii, viii, ix, x, xi, xii, xvi, xviii, 50, 51, 52, 53, 56, 57, 60, 72–76, 77, 82, 84–85, 92, 93, 95, 96, 101–104, 109, 112, 113, 116, 121, 151

Iti, Tame 52, 62

Iuli, Mapu xvi, 56, 111, 112, 113, 114, 115, 116

Iuli, Ta xvi, 38, 53, 104–106, 151

Jackson, George vi, 90

Jackson, Hana 93

Jackson, Syd 52, 62, 76, 93

Jones, Anna 76

Junior Nigs 53, 54, 64 see also Nigs

Karangahape Road 9, 28, 29–30, 105, 150

Kestle, Mrs 8, 9

King Cobras 32

Kingsland 58, 59, 109

Kirk, Norman 28

Kohitere 33, 35

Kuala Lumpur x

Lange, David xvi, 52, 59, 72–76, 88, 108

Lavulavu, Coral 76

Lepo, Brian 70

Levertov, Denise 104

Levin Boys' Training Centre 33

Lolly, Sione (John Minto) 71, 72

Luafutu, Fa'amoana John (Foof) xvi, 3–11, 30–44

Luafutu, Losa 4, 11

Ludbrooke, Robert xvi, 76–77, 88

Macintyre, Duncan viii

Macpherson, A.J.C. x

Malcolm X 24, 56, 90

Mandela, Nelson 62, 101

Mangere 9, 30, 51, 63, 75

Manurewa 9

Marley, Bob 66

Matafeo, Jake 70

Matafeo, John 70

Maung, Bill 58

Maung, David 61

McLeod, Eddie 76

Meanata, Elizabeth xvi, 111, 112, 113, 114, 115, 116, 121

Meanata-Montgomery, Mere xvi, 112, 113, 114, 115, 116

Minto, John (Lolly, Sione) 71, 72

Mt Albert Grammar School (MAGS) 24, 25, 53, 80, 150

Mt Eden prison 25, 80

Muldoon, Robert xi

INDEX

National Council of Churches ix, 88, 90

National Youth Council xii

Nee Nee, Henry vii, 50, 66

Nesian Mystic 71

Ness, Tigi (Tigilau) xii, xvi, xviii, xix, 25, 55–60, 62, 108–109

New Lynn vii

New Zealand Race Relations Council ix, xi, 77

New Zealand Social Services Council xii

New Zealand Student Christian Movement xi, 97

Newnham, Tom xvi, xvii, 52, 80, 108

Newton, Huey P. xiii, xiv, xvi, xxi, 78, 90

Ngā Tamatoa vii, viii, ix, x, xi, xvi, 49, 52, 64, 66, 76, 77, 82–85, 88, 95, 97, 108, 114

Nigs 47, 48, 63, 71
    see also Junior Nigs

Noble, Lenora xvi, 112, 114, 115

O'Dwyer, Don 7

Onehunga ix, 90

Otahuhu 59, 109

Otara 30, 51, 53, 63, 64, 77, 82, 83

Owairaka Boy's Home 31, 32

Pacific Islanders' Church (PIC) 6, 16, 29, 90

Pacific Islanders (NZ) Association vii

Pakuranga 71

Papatoetoe 63

Papua New Guinea viii, 91

Paremoremo prison vii, x, 48, 61, 62, 63, 78, 93

Pasadena Intermediate School 7

Peach, Blair 89

People's Union vii, x, xi, xvi, xviii, 61, 62, 63, 64, 66, 69, 71, 77–79, 88
    see also Ponsonby People's Union

Pereira, David 7

Point Chev (Point Chevalier) 65

Police Task Force xi, 59, 71, 78, 81, 82

Polynesian Education Foundation vii

Ponsonby v, vi, vii, viii, ix, x, xi, xii, xviii, 1, 9, 18, 19, 23, 24, 25, 27, 28, 29, 30, 32, 35, 36, 37, 39, 40, 41, 42, 43, 44, 48, 49, 51, 52, 54, 55, 59, 61, 63, 64, 65, 67, 69, 75, 76, 77, 78, 83, 88, 91, 93, 95, 101, 105, 107, 111, 112, 113, 115, 116, 151

Ponsonby Community Association 76

Ponsonby People's Union xi, 77

Pouesi, George 25

Poutasi, Samoa 4, 6, 11, 34

Rauhihi, Ama vii, viii, ix, x, 55, 62, 79, 88, 90

Reid, Paul 25

Richards, Trevor 52

Richmond Road Primary School 25

Rickard, Eva 109

Robinson, Sir Dove-Myer vi, viii

Saifiti, Atenai (Nai) 5, 7, 8, 9, 10, 32

Saifiti, Piko 5, 32

Saifiti, Puaa 5, 7, 8, 9, 10, 30, 31, 32, 33, 34, 35

Saifiti, Sa 4, 5

Saifiti, Tupulua 4, 5, 9, 10

Samoa xxi, 3, 5, 7, 15, 17, 21, 22, 34, 40, 44, 83, 102, 109, 120, 148

Sanft, Vaughn 52

Scanlan, Joe 32

Schmidt, Etta xvi, 56, 66, 67–69, 111, 121

Schmidt, Fred (Captain Fred) xvii, 38, 40, 41, 42, 43, 44, 52, 67, 68, 69, 111

Scribe 71,104

Seddon High School viii, ix, 31, 58

Sefuiva, Sam xvi, 111, 112, 113, 114, 115, 116

Sesega, Ness xvi, 109–111

Shadbolt, Tim 56
Sheperd, Dave 7
'The Shillouette' xvi, 24–25, 53–55
Singapore x
South Africa vi, vii, 68, 79, 80, 82, 84, 89, 92
South Auckland x, xix, 36, 48, 53, 63, 75, 94, 95
St Joseph's Convent School 6
Stanley, Gordon xvii
Stevens, Mike 96
Stewart, Mr 10, 31
Stormtroopers vii, 49, 63
Sutherland, Oliver 52, 108
Sydney viii, 48, 50
Sykes, Bobby viii, viii

Tahu, Tom vi
Tamati, Victor xvi, 94–95, 101, 103
Taylor, Esther 96
Te Atatu 30
Te Roopu o te Matakite xii
Teavae, Nooroa vii, xvii, 38, 66
Tihei Mauriora vii, 49
Tokomaru Bay vii
Toleafoa, Alec xvi, xix, 23–24, 107
Toleafoa, Wayne vii, xvi, 50–53, 93, 121
Tonga ix, xxi, 25, 82, 83, 85, 91, 93, 96, 101, 102, 160
Tuiasau, Fuimaono Norman xvi, 89–94
Tuiavati, Henry 24
Tuisamoa, Agnes xvii, 70, 109
Tuisamoa, Vincent xvi, 70–72, 109

United Kingdom 28, 89, 102
United States vi, xi, xiv, xviii, 28, 40, 50, 51, 56, 61, 62, 77, 90 94, 101, 104, 105, 120

University of Auckland iv, x, xi, xix, xx, xxi, 11, 18, 20, 45, 56, 83, 85, 90
University of Otago 96, 97

Vietnam viii, 24, 69, 77, 83, 89, 91, 112
Vilisoni, Lito 55–60

Waikeria borstal 62, 78
Waipouri 96
Waitangi 48, 49, 62, 91, 93
Walker, R. 45
Wallace, Vicki 67
Wallace, Zac 67
Wark, Betty 61, 76, 109
Wehi, Aloma xvi, 103, 111, 112, 113, 114, 115, 121
Wehrmacht 36, 39
Wellington iv, xi, 6, 64, 93, 96, 100, 122
Wells, Robby 7
Wendt, Albert 15, 24, 25
Williams, Eddie xvii, 50, 52, 66, 121
Williams, Mark 55
West Auckland 63, 64, 65
    see also names of suburbs
Western Springs 7, 31, 5